ROCK YOUR LIFE

ROCK YOUR LIFE

Encouraging Stories to Inspire and Motivate You to Rock Your Life

CRAIG DUSWALT

HYBRID GLOBAL PUBLISHING

Published by
Hybrid Global Publishing
301 E 57th Street, 4th Floor
New York, NY 10022

Manufactured in the United States of America, or in the United Kingdom when distributed elsewhere.

ISBN: 978-1938015-80-9 (hardcover)
ISBN: 978-1938015-81-6 (eBook)

Cover design: Joe Potter
Cover Photoshop work: Joe Potter
Interior design: Claudia Volkman
Typesetting: Claudia Volkman
Craig Duswalt photo: Robert John
Rock Your Life Logo Design: Dianne Porter

Disclaimer: The purpose of the book is to educate and entertain. The authors or publisher does not guarantee that anyone following the techniques, suggestions, tips, ideas, or strategies will become successful. The authors and publisher shall have neither liability or responsibility to anyone with respect to any loss or damage caused, or alleged to be caused, directly or indirectly by the information contained in this book.

www.CraigDuswalt.com
www.RockStarMarketingBootCamp.com
www.RockYourLifeNight.com

DEDICATION

This book is dedicated to everyone who wants to live more,
love more, and laugh more.
To the dreamers and the world changers, I salute you!
Rock Your Life!

Introduction

This book, along with my Rock Your Life TV YouTube Channel and my Rock Your Life World Tour, have been a lifelong dream. And I'm happy to say, it's all finally coming together.

In 2007, I started as a speaker, teaching marketing to entrepreneurs. I grew very fast in the industry, and immediately started a very successful coaching program, where I help businesses become known as experts in their fields through my RockStar Marketing BootCamps, my exclusive RockStar Master-Mind meetings, and through private coaching calls.

But, while my expertise is in marketing, I found that most people wanted to talk to me about their lives. They wanted to learn more about how to balance business and pleasure, and how to balance work and family.

And that was when I realized that I needed to take my marketing business to the next level, and introduce my new brand, Rock Your Life, to the masses. So now, not only do I teach marketing, and how to become more successful in business, and how to make more money, but now I enjoy helping people become more successful in LIFE. Teaching people how to Rock Their Lives!

This book is the launch of the brand. I found sixty-eight amazing people to share their stories, so that you will learn how to Rock Your Life!

Enjoy the ride.

Craig Duswalt
2017

Author Photo Credits

Alan Skidmore — Yoti Telio
Alex Lanshe — Sofia Vober
Anne/Anton Duswalt — N/A
Barbara Starley — Elaine Kessler
Bart Rademaker, MD — N/A
Bill Walsh — N/A
Briana Dai — Samantha Jane Creative
Captain Charlie Plumb — Paul Mobley
Chris Kopf — Val Westover
Chris McLean, MA — N/A
Craig Batley — John Bloom Custom Photography
Craig Duswalt — Robert John
Crystal Meisner — Val Westover
Darrell Griffin — Val Westover
David Medansky — Val Westover
David Nassaney — Val Westover
Dean Cain — N/A
Debbie McCormick — Stephanie Adriana Westover
Debbie Morgan — Yoti Telio
Deborah Kagan — Jeff Xander
Don Cromwell — Oscar G. Elizondo
Dr. Ellen Contente — Jaime Alysen Contente-Pelayo
Dr. Jay Shetlin — Val Westover
Dr. Theodoros Kousouli — Matthew A. Cooke
"Famous Dave" Anderson — Mark Lundeen
Gary Howarth — Val Westover
George Partsalidis — Sutton Group
Geri England — J. C. Penny Portraits
Hepsharat Amadi, MD — Jim Harris
Janie Lidey — Val Westover
Jeffrey Wolfe — Val Westover

Joel Weldon — Brad Hall
Judy Schriener — Ed Vanderlee
Karen Strauss — Stephanie Adriana Westover
Ken Courtright — Gayle Dawn
Kerri Courtright — Tom Stephenson
Linda Fleischmann — Jody Ross
Linda Hodge — Dennis Waller
Linda Kruse — Cutter Cutshaw
Lori Zapata — Lori Zapata
Maryann Ehmann — Barbie Santos
Melinda Stallings — N/A
Melody Keymer Harper — Val Westover
Michelle Calloway — Studiobooth
Miguel Sanchez — Lesley Bohm
Miss Winnie — N/A
Natasha Duswalt — Val Westover
Neecol Resnin — Val Westover & Stephanie Adriana Westover
Nola Aronson — Lindsay Helen Schlick
Patricia Karen Gagic — Derek van der Kolk
Paul Barbe — Tim Trerise
Paul Finck — Adam Sternberg
RADM Paul Becker — Sherilyn Kosuda Luke
Ray Parker Jr. — David Ochoa
Russell Hitchcock — Denise Truscello
Sandra Yancey — Jin Kim
Scott Transue — Val Westover
Scott Zimmerman — Ed Ouellette
Stephen Carpenter — Eva Russel Canaya
Steve Love — Val Westover
Susan Sheppard — Stephanie Adriana Westover
Suzy Prudden — Mary Ann Halpin
Terri Hardin — Lucia Sullivan
Tesy Ward — John D. Ward
Tim Gillette — Val Westover
TK O'Geary — Val Westover
Vivian R. England — Nikkia Redd
Walt Grassl — Val Westover

CONTENTS

WE ALWAYS WANT MORE!

Craig Duswalt

I have lived a blessed life—a very blessed life. Were there struggles? Of course. But I have worked hard my entire life, I've kept a positive attitude even during the down times, and I have been rewarded. I currently run a very successful speaking and coaching business. I'm married to my amazing soulmate, Natasha, and I have three intelligent and compassionate boys. My sister and her family are amazing, and my mom and dad are still here to give their loving advice to me, and listen when I need to share. My personal life is amazing.

Life is a wonderful thing. But as a society, we always want more.

Ten years ago, at forty-five years old, I started a new career as a speaker. I am a perfect example that it's never too late to follow your dreams. My RockStar Marketing BootCamps, held every March and September in Los Angeles, have been a dream come true. We average 300 to 400 attendees every six months, and I have an incredible group of world changers in my exclusive RockStar Marketing MasterMind Group. My business life is amazing as well.

But we always want more.

I've written eight books over the past ten years, and I have spoken on large stages all around the world. I've coached thousands of people on how to market their businesses better than their competition, and it felt really great. I love helping people.

But we always want more.

About six years ago I invested in a new musical written by two friends of mine in hopes that it would someday end up on a Broadway stage. I have a theatre background, and I've always wanted to be involved in putting on plays. When I lived in Santa Clarita, California, I opened an eighty-one-seat Equity Waiver theatre called the Repertory East Playhouse, and it was an incredible experience. I owned the theatre for a few years, but it was just a stepping-stone for something bigger, and that's why I invested in the musical, *The Honeymooners*, based on the hit television series with Jackie Gleason and Art Carney. And rumor has it, as of the writing of this book, it's going to Broadway some time in 2018. I hope to see you all there.

But we always want more.

For years I have wanted to put on a one-night event where I could encourage, inspire, motivate and entertain people all over the world. Since I came from the music industry, I envisioned it would be kind of like a world tour in venues in major cities. I had been on numerous world tours with Air Supply and Guns N' Roses, but this time it was going to be *me* on the "big" stage.

So, for the first time in a long while, fear set in.

It's extremely weird that fear would enter my mind, because as I mentioned, I already put on large Bootcamps twice a year, and I speak to corporations, networking groups, associations, colleges, and at very large entrepreneur events all over the world. This is easy for me. But for some reason, I have this block about this specific event—this wonderful night of encouragement, inspiration, motivation, entertainment, and music.

As part of my talks, I consistently teach people how to overcome their fears. And I'm really great at helping others overcome fear, but I haven't been able to get that point across to myself for this one specific project.

I announced back in 2016 that I was going to launch my Rock Your Life Tour that year, but it never happened. I kept making excuses: I'm too busy, I'm writing another book, I'm speaking on too many stages. . . . All true, but just a bunch of excuses designed to not have to face my fear.

No more excuses!

So I finally did what I tell everyone else to do when they're having a hard time making a commitment—I scheduled a date, and I told the world about it.

The new event is called Craig Duswalt's Rock Your Life Night, and it is based on this book you're reading and on my Rock Your Life TV YouTube channel. But I didn't just schedule a date at a typical venue that "we speakers" speak at. I didn't book a hotel, or a community room, or a school theatre, or a Chamber of Commerce boardroom. Instead I booked a night at the City National Grove of Anaheim in Anaheim, California. This is a place where big concerts take place and big names play. It even shares a parking lot with Angel Stadium where the Los Angeles Angels of Anaheim baseball team plays. The venue has a box office, a security team, a stage manager, a lighting designer, a sound designer, a production team, ushers, and everything else you would expect when you go to a concert. It's the real deal.

And I will be performing there on November 4, 2017, with some very influential friends. Yes, I, Craig Duswalt, will be on the same stage where numerous RockStars have stood before me, and I will finally be sharing my inspirational messages with a huge crowd.

Am I still scared? You bet I am. But I do not want to live with regret, and I'd rather take the chance of failing than never try.

Too many people have gone to their graves with their story inside them and have not left their legacy on this earth. And I just think that's so sad. So I will not be that person.

And I will not fail. I am so excited for this new event. I've put together an amazing team of people to help me, and it will be a huge success, and I will tour the world with this amazing show. There, I said it. Think positive, right?

And I will not stop there. While I have been very comfortable the past ten years, putting on successful events, speaking on large stages, and making a good living, I'm done being "comfortable."

Because we always want more. Everyone always wants more. And that's OK. As long you're nice to people along the way, and you work hard, and you live life with passion, and you genuinely want to help people, you will get more. In fact, I believe you will get whatever you want, as long as you GO FOR IT!

So, look out Broadway, here I come!

Craig Duswalt is a Speaker, Author, Podcaster, and the creator of the brands RockStar Marketing and Rock Your Life.

Craig's background includes touring with Guns N' Roses, as Axl Rose's personal assistant, and Air Supply, as the band's personal assistant.

Craig was also an award-winning copywriter, working as a Creative Director for a Los Angeles-based ad agency until opening up his own ad agency, Green Room Design & Advertising, which was named the 2002 Santa Clarita Valley Chamber of Commerce Small Business of the Year.

Craig combined his backgrounds in both music and marketing, and now teaches entrepreneurs, small businesses, authors, speakers and coaches how to promote themselves and their business by thinking outside the box at his 2 1/2-Day RockStar Marketing BootCamps every March and September in Los Angeles.

Craig delivers a very high-energy presentation, filled with useable content, interesting videos, exciting music, and extremely unique (never heard before) stories from his days touring with Guns N' Roses, and Air Supply, and his days working with corporate giants including Baskin Robbins, Los Angeles Dodgers, ESPN, and the Academy Awards just to name a few.

Craig Duswalt speaks at seminars, associations, networking groups, conferences and colleges, teaching entrepreneurs how to use outside the box marketing techniques to attract clients, and how to stand out from the competition — Like a RockStar. Craig is also a very popular Corporate Keynote Speaker.

Craig has written eight books, and is finally launching his Rock Your Life World Tour in 2017!

www.CraigDuswalt.com

I'M STILL STANDING

Russell Hitchcock

I was born in East Brunswick, Victoria, Australia, in 1949. We lived in the inner city between a brickworks and an iron foundry. My parents provided for my sister and I as best they could, and in spite of not having a lot of money, we always had a roof over our heads and food on the table. My childhood was uneventful except for being struck by a pickup while crossing an intersection as I walked to school. Apart from a badly bruised hip, I was fine. My mother however, being the comic that she was, told practically everyone up until the day she died that "Russell wasn't right in the head after he got hit by the truck!"

The work ethic I have today is due to my parents. They both worked, and I cannot remember either one of them ever missing a day's work. It was always instilled in us that hard work and perseverance would ultimately pay off later in life.

I attended grade school and eventually moved on to Princes Hill High School. I was an average student—I loved French and English but not much else during those years. I was too interested in having fun rather than studying. My drive to succeed in life began when I dropped out of high school at sixteen years of age. I received my exam results on a Friday, and having failed, I realized that repeating the year would be a waste of my parent's hard-earned money. I told my mother I was done, and the next day I went into the city, where I saw a sign in a small clothing store advertising for a "junior salesman." I walked in, applied, and was given the job on the spot! One of the things I've been proud of all my life is that since the age of sixteen, I have supported myself.

It wasn't until 1975, after having a number of jobs in the intervening years (I was never fired), that I found myself in the Australian production of *Jesus Christ Superstar*. On May 12th I met Graham Russell, and my life would never be the same.

We quickly became friends, realizing just how much we had in common, most of all a fanatical love for the music of the Beatles. We had both seen them live in 1964, Graham in England and me in Australia. Graham has always had great passion for the music he writes, and I've always felt I was the perfect fit to sing his songs. It wasn't long before we were performing together in coffee bars, pizza parlors, and the occasional university campus. We worked very hard

4

to become as good as we could, and Graham, very early on, was determined to be ready when the production ended.

By the time the show ended in October 1976, we had a number one single and album in Australia, and we went on the road as Air Supply only a few days after leaving *Jesus Christ Superstar.*

We played anywhere we could—a lot of pubs that were hard-core rock 'n' roll venues and among the premier acts at the time, AC/DC, Midnight Oil, INXS, and the Angels. Needless to say, playing mostly ballads was a hard road to hoe, but in those early days, it gave us an invaluable lesson in mental toughness, perseverance, and patience.

Early in 1977 we were invited to open for Rod Stewart in Australia. When you consider that Air Supply was only three months old, it was an amazing achievement. Playing to over twenty thousand people a night was overwhelming, but it was such a great incentive for us to broaden our horizons and seek international success. We knew we had the talent and the songs and would not be denied our shot. After only a couple of shows, Rod asked us to open for him on his North American tour later that year. We were ecstatic and believed this would be our stepping-stone to international stardom. We toured with Rod from September through December, playing fifty-plus concerts in all the venues we'd only dreamed about: Madison Square Garden, The Forum in Los Angeles, Candlestick Park, and Three Rivers Stadium. It was mind-blowing!

One of the greatest gifts we received from Rod was being able to watch him every night. We would marvel not only at his talent as a singer, but also the way he handled the audiences, taking them where *he* wanted them to go. We learned so much from him about performing, production, organization, and in fact, every aspect of the business. We soaked it up, absorbing as much as we could, and by the time we arrived back in Australia in December, we thought we were going to break on a worldwide scale.

How wrong we were! Coming off the biggest tour of the year and coming home to the brutal fact that we'd basically been forgotten by the public was not only shocking to us considering what we'd achieved, but it also made us more determined to achieve the goals we had set in those very early days. Rejection can do one of two things. Either it can cause you to give up and go home, or in our case, to say to ourselves, "We have the talent, the songs, the drive, and the passion to continue," and that's exactly what we did.

We struggled through the next couple of years doing whatever we could to survive. Graham ended up in Cannes trying to sell his songs, and I was in Australia doing "jingles" for a friend who was kind enough to hire me. During this time, though, with Graham's fearless determination and incredible vision, we kept our dreams alive until 1978 when "Lost in Love" was released in Australia and once again, we had a huge hit on our hands. The song made its way to Clive Davis at Arista Records in the United States. Clive, in my opinion is the most influential person that has ever been in the recording business, and he *loved* our songs. We had seven Top Five singles back-to-back, and we were on top of the world.

Becoming successful is one thing, but maintaining it is another. We toured incessantly to support our records, playing all over the world and even in places that very few acts had been, such as South Korea, Vietnam, Thailand, Malaysia, and a host of other countries both in Asia and Latin America. We worked extremely hard (and still do) to achieve and maintain the highest level of concert performance. Graham is always looking to make the shows better and looking at the arrangements of the songs to involve the influences of the current members of the band, while of course maintaining the integrity of the songs. We want our audiences to hear what they come to hear and not some vague version of the songs they know and love.

We will never stop trying to get better, and this desire has made it possible to still be on the road after forty-two years and counting. You can always do better, be better and achieve any goal you put your heart and soul in. You must stay focused and even through adversity, rejection, and hard times stick to your beliefs and know that you will succeed and continue to do so as long as you have the passion.

Having such a brilliant writer, arranger, and prolific composer has certainly made it easier for us, but trust me, we've seen it all. We've seen the good, the bad, and the ugly in people, but we've never succumbed to the dark side of the music business. I am as excited today as I have ever been in my life about recording and performing and hopefully have some great years ahead of me.

As I frequently say to friends and fans . . . ROCK ON!

Russell Hitchcock is the lead singer of the extremely successful rock duo, Air Supply. Air Supply hits include "Lost in Love," "All Out of Love," "The One That You Love," "Sweet Dreams," "Making Love Out of Nothing At All," "Here I Am," "Even the Nights Are Better," "Every Woman in the World," "The Power of Love," "Just As I Am," and "Two Less Lonely People in the World." With seven top-five singles, Air Supply, at the time, equaled the Beatles' run of consecutive top five singles. Air Supply albums, *Lost in Love, The One That You Love, Now and Forever,* and *Greatest Hits* have sold in excess of 20 million copies. *Lost in Love* was named Song of the Year in 1980, and, with the other singles, sold more than 10 million copies. Air Supply has continued to tour around the world for more than forty years.

www.AirSupplyMusic.com

MAN OF STEEL

Dean Cain

I'm 8 years old and playing in my first-ever organized basketball game. The kid guarding me is much quicker—everywhere I turn, he's already there, like an annoying gnat. Finally, I grab him by the shirt and throw him to the ground. Whistles blow and parents complain. My dad turns to my mom and says, "Maybe he should play football."

For the next 14 years, my mettle was hammered out on the gridiron. I didn't have time or interest in drugs or other distractions, because I was too focused. Football helped me get into Princeton University, where I became an All-American and briefly made it to the NFL with the Buffalo Bills (knee injury . . . a different book). Football helped me make friends, because having 110 teammates ensures plenty of diversity and challenges and close interaction. Football helped me vent and channel frustration and aggression and anger into hard work, discipline, and ultimately, success.

I love athletics. They tell you so much about a person's character. What kind of teammate are you? How do you react to adversity? Are you coachable? How do you respond when you're tired, or sick, or injured, or under tremendous pressure? How do you react to a bad call? This is not to say that people *have* to play sports (my own son doesn't play team sports—he trains in mixed martial arts), but athletics were essential to my overall development.

I love competition. Growing up, I played every sport under the sun. Four and five sports a year, all year 'round for 15 years. I learned how to win. I learned how to lose. I learned how to get back up after being knocked down. I learned that everyone gets knocked down. Everyone. I was voted top athlete in my high school. I was voted top athlete at my college. I lettered in 3 different sports at Princeton, but no sport could hold a candle to my love for football.

I love contact. In high school, my football/track coach said, "Cain, you're the only guy I know who runs FASTER when he HITS the hurdles!" In college, I ran my 40-yard-dash faster with my gear on. Running without my helmet and shoulder pads felt awkward, like a knight without his armor. Football was a great fit for me, but the road to RockStar success is never easy.

I wanted to kill my college football coach. Literally. Before my sophomore year at Princeton, the head coach was fired. Under the new regime, I tried to switch from defensive back to receiver but was quickly sent back to the defense. They never had any intention of letting me play offense. My new defensive back coach was called "Vermin." That wasn't his real name, but that's what a few of us called him. It was not a term of endearment.

As the only sophomore starting on the defense, and starting at cornerback, Vermin let me know that opposing teams would be targeting me. He let me know this every day, every practice, every meeting. He would scream at me all day long, until his voice went hoarse (which I took as a small victory). Vermin drove me and drove me and yelled at me—right in my face, EVERY SINGLE DAY. I took to staring defiantly into his beady little eyes, silent, and stone-faced. Vermin wouldn't let me drop a single ball in practice. EVER. Every pass in the air he expected me to intercept. Every tackle he expected me to make. This dude was all over me. As the season wound down, I was considering leaving Princeton and taking one of the many scholarships that had been offered to me out of high school (the Ivy League does NOT give athletic scholarships).

My dad flew to Princeton from the jungles of Brazil to catch the final game of my sophomore season. Dad had been directing a film for 6 months in the middle of the Amazon, had grown a jungle beard, and contracted malaria (he hadn't realized that yet). He didn't have time to go home to see my mother or the rest of the family in California. He had missed all my games (there was no Internet back then), and he wasn't gonna miss this last one. I talked with my tanned, skinny, and bearded dad about Vermin and all the crap he had put me through. Dad patiently gave me some sage farm-boy advice (he was raised on a farm in South Dakota). Then he told me to finish up the season and the semester, and afterward we'd discuss transferring to another school if I still wished.

We played Cornell the next day, and I faced off with their stud All-Ivy receiver. He was big and strong, and supposed to dominate me. We had a war all afternoon, and with time winding down they were driving for the winning score. They threw to the stud, but I stepped in front and picked it off for the *third* time of the day! I weaved my way through defenders and stepped out of bounds, sealing the victory! My teammates hoisted me onto their shoulders. RockStar!

I stayed at Princeton and continued to excel at defensive back. Junior year I was moved to free safety, where I really belonged. Vermin continued to ride me like a donkey, but I was getting tougher. The team had a terrible year, but I had another great season. The individual recognition felt hollow because the team hadn't won. As my senior season was about to begin, our beloved head coach suffered a heart attack and died. It was a devastating loss.

My family decided to move to Princeton for my senior season. They went to every single game, home and away. My father had just gotten his biggest break in Hollywood and was preparing to direct the film *Young Guns*. He was traveling back to Los Angeles during the week and then returning to Princeton for the weekend games. It was awesome to have their support. I was having the greatest season any defensive back had ever had in college football, and Vermin and I had made peace. I realized Vermin was like the character "Fletcher" that J. K. Simmons had won an Academy Award for playing in the film *Whiplash*. Vermin had driven me that hard to make me great. (Today we are still great friends, and Vermin continues to coach football at Princeton.)

The final game of my college career was at Princeton. Cornell again. My entire family was there. My girlfriend was there. It was the coldest game anyone could remember. With the wind-chill factor, it was -20 Fahrenheit. My sister still complains that it permanently screwed up the circulation in her feet (they were blue, and a woman had to put them inside her fur coat). At the end of the first half, I intercept my 10th pass of the season to leave me one interception shy of the single-season NCAA record (11). In the third quarter, a pass bounces off the chest of a Cornell receiver and directly into my hands! I've tied the record! I run it back, get knocked out of bounds on our sideline, and promptly make my way over to the stands. I toss the ball to my father. He throws it back. I throw it back harder and tell him, "That's for *you!*"

That moment is still my all-time favorite sports highlight. After all the blood, sweat, tears, fights with Vermin, and separation from my family, I got to tie the NCAA record and throw that football to my dad in the stands. I was finally a friggin' RockStar! Later in the game, I intercepted another pass, and broke the NCAA record for interceptions in a single season and became a SuperRockStar! Two of those NCAA records still stand, and my dad still has his football.

Dean Cain grew up in Malibu, California, and has appeared in over 100 films, including *Out of Time*, opposite Denzel Washington, *God's Not Dead*, *The Broken Hearts Club*, *Vendetta*, and the soon-to-be-released *Gosnell*. Dean has also starred in dozens of television productions and is perhaps best known for his role as Superman on ABC's *Lois & Clark*. He hosted and produced the long-running series *Ripley's Believe It Or Not*. Known for his incredible work ethic, Dean is currently starring in a wide array of projects, including the third season of VH1's hit series *Hit the Floor*, recurring on the widely popular CBS series *Supergirl,* and hosting the third season of the CW smash *Masters of Illusion*. An accomplished screenwriter, Dean has recently penned a number of screenplays which are in various stages of production. An athlete at heart, Dean attended Princeton University, and was an All-American defensive back, setting two NCAA records for interceptions. He signed with the Buffalo Bills, but a knee injury quickly ended his professional sports career before it had begun.

Twitter: @RealDeanCain

A HIGH SCHOOL BREAK

Ray Parker Jr.

One big jump in my career came when I was seventeen years old. It was just a few weeks before my eighteenth birthday. I was in college studying to be an architect so I could work for one of the big three in Detroit. It was my father's dream to have me work at Ford Motor Company, as he did. My dad worked at Ford for forty-eight years as a crane operator. His big dream for me was to have a white-collar job instead of a blue-collar job like his. I was attending Lawrence Tech College in the drafting department. I was bored out of my mind and well aware that this was probably not the right path for me. But it was my father's dream, and he had been saving money for my college education for years before I was born. I had already established myself as a working musician by this time and was enjoying it. I had been recording with many major artists like Marvin Gaye, Smokey Robinson, Honey Comb, the Spinners, and the Temptations.

Music for My Mind was my favorite album at the time. I had an eight-track tape player in my car, and it was the only album I listened to. One day I got a call from someone claiming to be Stevie Wonder! I knew it had to be one of my friends, so I hung up the phone. This person called back, and I hung up again. He then called back, and I added a few four-letter words before hanging up again. The next time he called, he asked me to listen. He played the beginning track to "Superstition"!

I finally understood that I had been hanging up on Stevie Wonder, so I apologized and listened. He said that he'd heard about me and wanted to know if I would be interested in going on tour with him and the Rolling Stones for several months, as well as work on his new album, *Talking Book*, and do some recordings with Crosby, Stills, Nash & Young!

This was certainly a great opportunity, and I really wanted to go. I told him of my situation with my father and said that I would have to get back to him. I then had the big sit-down conversation with my dad, telling him that this was his dream, not mine, and that I really wanted to go on tour. He explained how he wanted me to graduate college and be the first one in the family to do so. I had little interest. I was really frustrated with school anyway.

I had just finished a three-week-long drawing for class. I felt I had done a great job on the test, but I received a failing grade on a Friday evening. I sat up all weekend trying to figure out what was wrong. Because of the weekend I couldn't confront the teacher until Monday. When I did, she told me that my drawing was really impressive and the work was well done. She failed me because the arrows I used on the Ford car were GM specs, not Ford specs. For example, Ford arrows flared at the end and GM's didn't, even though the size was a slight difference. She explained to me that that's how things work at the Big 3.

I wanted out!

After talking with my father for quite some time, listening to what he had to say as well as letting him know that I was totally unhappy in school, he agreed to let me go on tour! I can't imagine where my life would be now if I'd stayed in school and took that path. This was a major turn to the left, and I've been happy ever since.

American guitarist, songwriter, producer and recording artist, Ray Parker Jr. is best known for writing and performing the theme song to the motion picture *Ghostbusters*, for his solo hits, and performing with his band Raydio as well as with the late Barry White.

Now, Parker enjoys spending time with his family while continuing his love and passion for music. He regularly performs in various concerts throughout the world.

www.RayParkerJr.com

NEVER GIVE UP

Don Cromwell

Being the son of a military career officer, an "Air Force brat" as we were known back then, my father constantly discouraged me from pursuing a career in the music business. When he accompanied me to purchase an acoustic guitar from Music Unlimited in San Leandro, California, at age fourteen, with eighty dollars of my own hard-earned money, he said, "It's fine for a hobby, D.R. [Donald Richard, named after his two brothers], just don't get too serious about it." I understood and didn't really give it much thought other than how much enjoyment I got out of playing music.

Fast-forward through the early years of playing school dances, parties, battles of the bands, local parks, and just about anywhere that would allow a live band, in 1973 I decided that music was indeed going to be my life pursuit. After my third year of college as a history major at Cal State Hayward, and at the invitation of a guitar player I knew from Oakland, I moved from the Bay Area to Seattle to join a band and give it a go, telling my mom I would be back to finish college if things didn't work out up north. Off I went in my VW van, determined to make my mark as a musician.

I was twenty years old and loved the sense of freedom and adventure. Dad wrote regular letters telling me I had made a bad choice and asking me to please reconsider what I was doing. Make no mistake, it hurt, but I felt music was my calling. After five years up in the Pacific Northwest, playing with several great bands but not making much progress in the business, I decided I needed to move back to California if I was to keep my career alive. Out of the blue I was offered the bass player position with a Top 40 band from Orange County that was regrouping. I accepted, packed my van (now a Ford Econoline with "three on the tree"), and headed south on I-5. It literally rained the entire drive from Seattle to the Oregon-California border, but when I got to the sign saying "Welcome To California," the rain suddenly stopped and the sun came out, shining brightly. I saw it as a sign from above, a very good sign, so I pulled the van over to the shoulder, stopped, got out, and kissed the ground. I was back home!

Our band was one of the top bands on the circuit, so we worked constantly and filled the clubs, which in turn led to more gigs and repeat bookings. It was a great group of musicians; we had a lot of fun and laughs together, as well as a large following. After a few months I purchased some recording equipment and set it up in the Buena Park rental house that I shared with two of the guys in the band. I spent a lot of time recording while learning the process, and I loved writing songs and putting them down on tape. I was improving both as a songwriter and musician, and I was more inspired than ever at this point.

A little more than two years after arriving in Southern California, and after a heartfelt conversation with a best friend at a San Diego Jack In The Box, I decided to leave the band. It wasn't easy telling my band mates that I was going to move on, but I had come back to Los Angeles to take my career to a higher level, and I knew I had to strike out on my own to achieve my goal. This led to some uneasy moments financially, as the band had provided a steady if not substantial paycheck, but it felt great to be independent and free to choose how I spent my time. To help ends meet, I would buy and sell used musical gear using a local paper called *The Recycler*. I soon was playing and creating with a vast array of musical talent, as well as connecting with a small independent record label and studio where I did a lot of writing and recording.

Dad was still "disappointed" in my chosen profession, of course, just about the worst word a child wants to hear from a parent. Who could blame him? I had nothing really to show for my efforts thus far, and it was coming up on ten years since I left the Bay Area to seek my fame and fortune. But Los Angeles was a center of the music business, along with New York and Nashville, and I just kept working hard and pressing on. While I certainly had regular moments of self-doubt and discouragement, I believed in myself and felt I was in the right place if I just stuck with my vision.

I had moved out of Orange County to be closer to the LA scene, and I heard through my roommate, also a musician, that Air Supply was in town auditioning for new band members. I knew the name but wasn't familiar with their music. On a Sunday night shortly thereafter, I was playing a show at a local club with one of several "project bands" I was involved with at the time, and when I walked in I noticed Graham Russell of Air Supply sitting in the audience. I found out later he was there to see the band after us, but timing and fate put me in front of him when I was playing with a great band.

I treated it like any other show, but when I finished, Graham came up to me and asked if I would like to audition, saying he had a partner in the band, the great vocalist Russell Hitchcock, and while he couldn't guarantee me the job, he felt I was what they were looking for. The audition went great, and I was called back twice, each time with a different group of musicians. After the third get together, Graham came up to me and asked, "Do you have a passport, mate? We'd love to have you join the band!"

The year was 1983, five years after moving to LA and ten years after leaving the Bay Area. Two weeks later we started a world tour in support of Air Supply's *Greatest Hits* album. The tour started in Japan and included two sold-out shows at Budokan in Tokyo. "Making Love Out of Nothing at All" was climbing the charts, and we were playing arenas and top venues at every stop. The effort, the hard work, and the patience had finally paid off. I felt at home in this environment and truly enjoyed the band, the crew, and the concert experience each and every day.

While in Japan, I noticed on the tour itinerary that our first show in the United States was at the Concord Pavilion, not far from San Leandro, where I grew up. I was already fired up to perform that night in front of a hometown crowd as we landed at Oakland Airport, and the first person I saw after getting off the plane was my father, holding up a sign that said, "Welcome, Air Supply." It brought tears to my eyes, and later that night, backstage after our concert, I had nearly fifty friends and family members whooping it up, making for a night I will never forget. Dad was beaming from ear to ear and was finally on board with my career. From that day on until his untimely passing in 1991, if we were in a restaurant he would always ask me if he could tell the waitress or waiter who I played with, and of course I said yes. It was the ultimate full circle for me, and I enjoyed his happiness more than my own.

I will always be grateful to Graham and Russell for the opportunity and for the hands of fate that brought us together for five amazing years of traveling the world playing music. But the smile on my father's face, knowing he was "proud of his son," telling me that the band was "better than Men At Work" and "someone should write a song called 'Take Time,'" and me finally writing that song in his honor—those are the victories and the memories I will cherish for a lifetime!

Don Cromwell is a professional producer/songwriter/musician based in Los Angeles. Originally from the East Bay Area in Northern California, Don spent several years in the Seattle music scene before relocating to Southern California. He became a fixture at the avant-garde label Unicorn Records, writing songs for and performing on many of their diverse releases.

From 1983 through 1987, Don toured as the bass player with the renowned pop group Air Supply. While with the band, he worked with top producers in the studio, co-wrote three songs on the hit album Air Supply, and appeared in numerous videos and television performances.

Following Air Supply, Don played bass with rock legend Eddie Money, touring and recording with him over the next six years. Don teamed up with long-time Eddie guitarist Tommy Girvin to form the group Ransom, releasing two well-received albums in Europe and Japan entitled *Trouble in Paradise* and *Better Days*.

After deciding to forego life on the road, Don has gone on to write and produce for Eddie Money, Jennifer Rush, Jana Anderson (of Stevie Nicks and Fleetwood Mac), and several top EMI Europe artists, and he produced Air Supply lead vocalist Russell Hitchcock's solo CD, *Take Time*.

He won the award for best producer at the 2016 Hollywood Music in Media Awards for his song "Where Do I Belong," and he has a weekly Internet radio show and podcast, *Don Cromwell LIVE*. Don still enjoys playing live whenever possible and has recently released the Carlsen-Cromwell CD *The Lucky Side*. He also has a successful real estate business and lives with his wife, Cindy, in Westlake Village.

www.facebook.com/don.cromwell

BEYOND SUCCESS

Natasha Duswalt

Success. The word has a range of meanings, a range of emotions and expectations. There are versions of success that we all seem to cling to as a cultural mass. Our friends and fellow travelers in the human experience look to each other for examples. Living in Los Angeles has a whole next level of success that escapes many. There are so many levels of success that at times it can feel like added pressure. Society creates new and innovative levels of success that really can resemble jumping through hoops. The question is: Which hoops define your success?

Success is inactive without faith. We all make plans. Faith is what activates those plans. You literally cannot step onto a plane without a level of faith that once it takes off you will arrive at a new destination. The same goes for any child born, relationship, business plan, book, coaching, musical endeavor, writing and producing a movie—they all require the faith that something is always moving forward. The key for me has been linking up my life purpose to the things I do daily. My life is about being present, living on purpose, helping others, and always being mindful of what I am doing. I am also mindful of what takes me off my path and what wastes my time. There is no added time in a day, so making the most of each day may be one of the biggest successes anyone can achieve. Remember, when you live your life on purpose, none of it really feels like work when it's what you want to do.

Success for me is being at the point where you realize that you are part of the greater good that everyone benefits from. Success is when you take the time to share your experiences, your hope, and your strength to build up others without expectations.

But *beyond success* is when you step out of your comfort zone and speak, write books, and take risks, knowing that your words (either written or spoken) will be part of an inspiration and possibly the catalyst that someone else needs to move forward with creating their dream. *Beyond success* is planting the seeds of possibility wherever you go with every person you meet.

17

My personal story of beyond success started with my modeling and talent agency, Peak Models & Talent.

Based in Los Angeles, Peak Models & Talent was created to help others while making a living in the arena I knew and loved most. The first thing I had to do was to be clear on my mission. I wanted to have a company where models were engaged in their passion within a safe arena, where their values were never compromised. The creation of Peak Models & Talent has been a catalyst that helped make it possible for our family to grow and thrive.

Owning a modeling agency for two decades has its perks and its pressures. Peak Models & Talent was my baby before my kids were born. The goal of the agency was always to "help others," but at times when dealing in an industry where everyone is looking for the next break, the next deal, the next role, or the next booking, things that normally would be business as usual can take on a different shade of intensity.

The driving principles that were rooted in the creation of Peak Models & Talent are alive and well today, navigating all aspects of the company. These success principles work because we work them.

Clarity of Purpose Early on when I started my adult life, I had the realization that I needed to revisit and rebuild my life. I needed to map out a strategy and define what I wanted. I had to be specific. I had to line up my life with my purpose. It would be empty if it was only about how to make money. We are in a time where anything is possible, but living on purpose is what I have found to be life-changing. With that in mind, Peak Models & Talent set out with a clear purpose grounded in service.

Service Peak Models & Talent is in the service industry. Serving talent and clients has always been the forefront of the company. Our mind-set is that we are here to help and be of service.

Integrity This industry calls for the utmost integrity. When booking models and talent, we have made it our policy to outline all of the rates and payments up front so that everyone is on the same page and there is no mystery going in.

Follow-Through With every project, all of the moving parts need to be addressed. Our attention to detail and follow-though does not end when the job is done. We make sure to get feedback and listen to our clients for tips on how we can improve.

Responsibility With any company there can be little things that may not go as planned. Our goal is to always take responsibility. Our clients are looking for solutions; we are that solution. If something does not go as planned, it is our job to make sure that we navigate that and take responsibility so we can improve.

The success of Peak Models & Talent is to be the best version of the company for the people around us. The greatest success, I believe, is to show up in life fully engaged, fully present, and willing to help others. There is always money to be made and bills to be paid, but the true measure of success is not how much money we have but how we showed up and helped others in the process. The joy is in the doing, not the outcomes. We all love the wins, the shiny stuff, but it is in the daily grind where we see what we are made of, how we react, and how we engage.

Today Peak Models & Talent has helped thousands of people work in a competitive industry where the rules are always changing. Our passion and consistent work is the result of great people coming together to share and create in the entertainment industry. Our success is grounded in solid principles and a love of helping others succeed. Our unique recipe of success is that we go above and beyond. In an industry that can be so difficult, we have always looked to be a bright light.

Natasha Duswalt is a published author and speaker, and the president and founder of Peak Models & Talent in Los Angeles. As an international model, Natasha has had the rare opportunity to travel all over the world in places including New York, Miami, Hong Kong, Japan, Taiwan, Mexico, and several other locations working with top designers and companies. Natasha has been featured on numerous television shows including *Baywatch* and *Growing Pains*, as well as the hit movie by Oliver Stone *The Doors*. She was also hired as an ESPN Spokesmodel and has appeared on numerous television commercials.

Natasha's strong sense for business, negotiating skills, industry relationships and reputation inspired her to open Peak Models & Talent. Since 1997 Natasha has been booking models and talent for numerous projects in the field of modeling, including fit models for the fashion industry, print models, commercial print models, catalogs, runway, showroom, along with theatrical and commercial productions. Peak Models & Talent has been touted as one of Los Angeles' top agencies, booking with high-end clients such as Guess, Forever 21, Six Flags Theme Parks, Kardashians, Kendall + Kylie, Intel, Nokia, Reebok, Disney, ABS Clothing, Skechers, Nike, Dell, Audi, Mercedes, Honda, Speedo, Tempur-Pedic Sleep Systems, Starbucks, Bebe, Wells Fargo, Honda, Patagonia, Princess Cruises, Tommy Bahama, Kmart and Target just to name a few.

Natasha is also a proud cancer survivor showing that nothing will stop her when it comes to living a life of purpose! Natasha's inspirational message will remind us what is possible and what we are capable of achieving. There is no limit once you realize that you are here for a limited time, and you were born with everything you need. Natasha currently lives in Los Angeles with her husband (speaker and author), Craig Duswalt, and their three children. Natasha's most recent book, *Women Who Rock* was a #1 Amazon Best-Selling book.

For speaking inquiries email Natasha@craigduswalt.com or Natasha@peak-models.com.

www.PeakModels.com

Don't Quit Five Minutes
Before the Miracle Begins

Sandra Yancey

When we look at wildly successful people, it's easy to be dismissive and make assumptions or projections, such as "They must have had it pretty easy," or "They must have had a backer," or "They must have been married to a spouse who funded them." The list goes on and on.

One thing I've learned in my eighteen years of helping entrepreneurs launch, grow, and scale their businesses is that behind the reality of great success are humbling moments of great despair.

It is the journey from despair to destiny that really shapes an entrepreneur.

Entrepreneurs who experience disappointment and disillusionment but never learn from them continue to struggle and often never live their dream. Entrepreneurs who accept, feel, and learn the realities of those tough moments; mourn their losses; seek meaning within them; and then build greatness using them are the ones who ultimately climb to the highest of heights.

Two years into my launch of eWomenNetwork, I was broke and broken. Coming off a really successful corporate career, the dire situation I found myself in really rattled me. I had never worked as hard in my life—for the least amount of money I had ever made. It shook me to the core, and it started playing with my mind and undermining my confidence. Raising two children under the age of eight, operating on about four hours of sleep a night, and taking on every job myself, I wondered, *Can I really do this?* In addition to being on the brink of bankruptcy, I was on the brink of quitting.

One day my mother called to chat and asked me how things were going. I remember standing at the door, looking outside, and thinking, *This day is so bright and beautiful, with such a gorgeous blue sky, yet inside I feel like I'm in the deepest storm ever.* I said to my mom, "I can't do this. I've got to find a job. I'll do eWomenNetwork on the side."

"Wait a minute," she said. "You're already working twenty hours a day. How are you going to get a job and expect this to work?"

Clouded by the fog of it all, I couldn't see her point of view. "Well, I really don't know, but I do know one thing: I can't pay my bills, and I've got to quit," I replied.

And then, like so many important times before, my mother's wisdom surfaced again and she asked me one poignant question: "How do you know you're not quitting five minutes before the miracle begins?"

I was quiet for a moment, and then said, "Well, I don't."

It was then that my mother really gave me the strength and power of outside forces. She said, "Well, honey, then you really can't quit. I'm not saying don't quit, but if you do quit, you have to know. You have to know that this is what you want to do and have to do. And you're not there yet. If you quit now, I promise you, you will spend the rest of your life wondering what might have been."

Her response really touched me, and I knew in my heart she was right, but the doubts lingered. "Then what do I do?" I said.

"I don't know," she replied. "But I know one thing: I raised a daughter smart enough to figure it out."

I was drowning, and with that simple statement, my mother reached in, pulled me out, and saved me. She gave me the confidence to take that one next step. In that moment, I realized that I didn't have to figure everything out right then; I just had to acknowledge that I didn't know, and then ask for help. After all, what was the worst thing that could happen?

You too may feel like you're drowning, wondering if you'll ever be able to make this dream of yours happen. You too may be tired, overworked, struggling to get by. You too may be ready to quit. I may not know how you will pull it off, but I do know two things for sure: You are smart enough to figure it out, and you are not alone.

I believe one of the biggest mistakes entrepreneurs make, myself included sometimes, is the shame when things aren't going well. We remain silent, carrying the heavy weight of this burden alone unnecessarily. The truth is, we have much to learn from people like you who had an idea, a dream, a goal, and when faced with challenges, turned barriers into benchmarks, obstacles into opportunities, and setbacks into stepping-stones—and succeeded in spite of it all. And many of these "other people" are much closer than you think.

Everyone I know who has built a seven-figure business and been able to sustain it has a network. This network consists of people in their life who give them strength when they are fatigued or a Band-Aid when they feel broken.

We all need others from time to time to spread some sunshine when we are in darkness. No one makes it alone. It is essential that you have a network of people to turn to for wisdom, inspiration, ideas, and insights.

You can't build a million-dollar dream hanging around minimum wage mind-sets. Take inventory of the people you spend time with on a regular basis. Do they inspire you or tire you? If they don't lift you up, bless and release them so that you give space to those who will. I know they are looking for you. Make sure you make yourself available so they can find you.

And when you're in the catbird seat, I hope you remember where you came from. I know I promise to continue to show up and assist someone else who needs guidance and support. Together we can help someone else to feel less alone and lift as we climb. Each of us share one important thing in common: We are but one resource away from the miracle beginning.

Sandra Yancey is an international award-winning entrepreneur, best-selling author, movie producer, and philanthropist who left her successful Fortune 500 corporate career to launch eWomenNetwork in 2000. Two years into her business, she was on the verge of bankruptcy and ready to close her doors. She now leads one of the most successful multimillion dollar business networks in North America. With 500,000 entrepreneurs connected to her network, the company produces one thousand events annually. CNN recognized Sandra as an American Hero because of her humanitarian outreach through her eWomenNetwork Foundation. Sandra is the preeminent women's business expert, leading entrepreneurs as they launch, grow, and scale their businesses.

www.eWomenNetwork.com

FORGIVING THE UNFORGIVABLE

Captain Charlie Plumb

I was really angry. Angry at my government for sending me to Vietnam, angry at myself for getting shot down, angry at my God for not sending a miracle angel to rescue my copilot and me when our supersonic F-4 Phantom was blown out of the sky by a surface-to-air missile. And perhaps, most of all I was angry with the enemy for the torture and brutality; the unbelievable physical pain they had brought to my body in clear violation of the Geneva Convention. I lay on the filthy prison floor and bled . . . and wept.

I had no idea, in that moment of misery and pain, the sweeping significance and indelible impact that experience was to have on the rest of my life. In fact, I was convinced that the most value this window of time could ever be would be a period of my life I could someday FORGET! It would take months of anguish to teach me a life-saving lesson. And even today, having had many years to reflect on the value of my POW experience, I'm still learning . . . and growing from being a prisoner of war for nearly six years in North Vietnam.

In some ways, my psychological response seemed to follow Kubler-Ross's model in her book *Death and Dying*. I can track her stages pretty clearly in my personal experience.

I began the first stage of denial having flown that world-class jet fighter through the skies of Vietnam for seventy-four successful combat missions, with only five days left of my tour of duty . . . I thought I was bulletproof. I couldn't believe the enemy had a gun big enough to shoot down Charlie Plumb. (The pain of the first bayonet stab in the back of my thigh quickly brought me out of that fantasy and into the next stage of *Death and Dying*.)

Kubler-Ross's second stage, anger, is where I dwelt the longest (and perhaps learned the most). It would take me years to finally understand and appreciate all this. At the time I really wanted to kill something . . . or someone. And I felt totally justified in that feeling. After all, by any intelligent analysis, I was the quintessential victim of circumstances beyond my control; twenty-four years old with a new wife back home, graduate of the Naval Academy with a great future ahead of me, I thought I had clearly been victimized by the fickle finger of fate.

But my simple formula for the most impactful lessons of life is this: L = PT. In order to really Learn something new, it takes a certain amount of Pain multiplied by a certain amount of Time. And for me this lesson took a considerable amount of physical and mental pain for about three months. That's how long it took for me to move on to the next stage. Kubler-Ross calls it acceptance. For me the psychological tool to implement acceptance is forgiveness.

An engineer by education, I tried to reason this through with a set of facts leading to a conclusion. My professors called it QED, from the Latin *quod erat demonstrandum*, or "thus it has been demonstrated."

First, I started to consider the consequences of my anger. It became pretty clear to me that no matter how much rage I could muster, I wasn't going to affect the outcome of the war (which had been, as a military guy, my primary mission). In fact, my personal wrath seemed to actually encourage and delight my captors. And, in harboring all this vitriol I was eating myself up—from the inside out! Assuming I still had the choice, it just didn't seem very profitable to harbor all these negative feelings.

So I found a new definition for anger. Using our secret prison-communication system, a fellow POW passed me this Mark Twain quote: "Anger is an acid that can do more harm to the vessel in which it is stored than to anything on which it is poured."

It took him several minutes to tap out that message through our mutual prison wall using our cumbersome code, but when I deciphered the final words and understood the meaning, I realized that I was that vessel. But even understanding that, the next question was to be the most daunting: If I can't pour the acid onto something, how on earth do I get rid of it? How do get the poison out of the vessel . . . my body? How do I change my attitude? How do I ignore the atrocities perpetrated on my fellow fighter pilots and me?

After much soul searching I found a simple tool. Simple to say but difficult to implement: unconditional forgiveness. It worked in the prison, and it works for me today. I heartily recommend it.

I had learned a lot about forgiveness from my mother. As a devout Christian, she practiced it daily. I tried to as well. But my POW experience taught me it's more than a kind, Christian thing to do—it's vital for self-preservation in life-threatening trauma and in the rigors of our daily life.

And it isn't just forgiving our enemies; sometimes it's forgiving our loved ones, and sometimes even ourselves. This, in turn gives us permission to step forward, take control, and move on with our lives. I'm convinced that we can imprison ourselves with blame, guilt, and self-doubt to the point that we are paralyzed. And those mental prison walls can be more restrictive than the ones of stone and steel that I was behind in the Vietnam prison camps. We can set ourselves free from those self-imposed chains when we implement unconditional forgiveness.

So the act of forgiveness can actually be a selfish one. (And I believe it's OK to be selfish once in a while.) In my experience, if you can maintain a forgiving heart, you can sustain a healthy heart.

So forgive the unforgivable . . . for the good of others, but mostly for yourself.

Charlie Plumb completed thirty-one years in the US Navy, retiring with the rank of captain. Since returning home, more than five thousand audiences in nearly every industry have been spellbound as Captain Plumb draws parallels between his POW experience and the challenges of everyday life. One of the most sought-after motivational speakers of his time, his presentations are as he is: sincere, straightforward, and humorous. In addition to delivering renowned keynote presentations, he proficiently creates and executes seminar workshops, safety stand-downs, and sessions for continuing education credits. To learn more about the speaker and the man, please visit his website.

www.CharliePlumb.com

HOW TO CONNECT WITH MILLIONAIRES AND BILLIONAIRES

Bill Walsh

As the CEO and founder of Powerteam International, for the past two decades my team and I have worked to produce educational programs for business owners, speakers, and high-level masterminds all over the world. I have three amazing children, Austin, Marissa, and Evan, and they are definitely my big WHY! I'm going to share with you some amazing secrets of how to connect with millionaires and billionaires. My realization of the process comes from doing it wrong for so many years!

How many times have you had the opportunity at a networking event, a meeting, or in a casual conversation to connect with someone who is extremely successful, and you're just not sure what to say? I'll tell you what most people say. They go, "Blah, blah, blah . . ."; they say something totally off; or they say nothing at all.

When you get a great chance to connect with high-level people, you need to know what to say, be on cue, and understand how to instantly build rapport. People that know how to create congruent rapport are the ones who win in the conversation. For instance, I met Michael Jordan in the Bahamas, and an hour later we were doing my Ice Bucket challenge video; an hour after that he was giving my kids tips on playing basketball. It is sad that many times people walk away or say nothing, and their chance of connecting is pretty much zero. I don't want you to miss those opportunities.

Here's rule number one: When you enter into the conversation, you need to stand out. You've got to figure out something that makes you stand out from everyone else there. It can be just the way you say hello, or the fact that you look them in the eye and shake their hand. Too often people meet successful entrepreneurs and right away want to talk about themselves. "Hi, my name is Joe and I'm in real estate; there are lots of deals for you . . ." It turns people off. They don't want to hear about it.

Another big mistake that people make is trying to give the guru their next great idea. Everyone wants the expert's help. They might say, "Hey, I'm new and investing in property—could you help me?" or "I'm just getting started in building my new business and I want to learn how to get venture capital. Can you help me?" Successful people back away from that. Now, they're not going to tell you this. They might even ask for your business card, but five minutes later it's in the trash.

You want to make a first impression that stands out. You've got to create that instant rapport with in that first twenty-nine seconds, because if you don't, you've lost that person. One of the best things to do is to get the experts to talk about themselves. Successful people like to talk about themselves. They like to talk about things that are happening in their world or their sphere. If you want to strike a chord that instantly allows them to know that you're actually interested in what they're doing, ask the expert what projects he or she is currently focused on. It encourages them to talk, and you can listen, learn, and process. Instead of thinking about yourself, when you have this opportunity, think about how can you serve that person, how you can create even more value in their life. When you come from a place of service, the universe will yield unlimited potential. Experts will feel your positive interest to truly serve and not be a taker. It's all about giving back and making a difference.

Think about ways you can get them talking about themselves, talking about things they are passionate about. It could be business or charity-related. You're looking for ways to tie it back to something you can do to provide value in the relationship. For example, if they have got a new book coming out or they've got a new event coming up, figure out ways you can help to spread the word. Instead of asking for things, ask what you can do.

Don't ever be afraid to approach successful people. Just go into the conversation having absolute confidence in what you do and how you can help them. When you are ready for success and willing to step outside your comfort zone, more success will show up for you. Here are three simple keys:

1. You've got to stand out.
2. You've got to be willing to talk about them.
3. You have to add value first and expect nothing in return.

Once I was in a meeting with a very, very successful individual. He usually does projects of more than $500 million and funds lots of business ventures. During that conversation, none of it was about me. I let him talk about himself and learned how to create value for him first. Fifteen years later we are still great friends.

Another time I had the chance to connect with Anthony Robbins. I was at a very high-level event for speakers, authors, and networkers from around the world. I was very fortunate to be invited to be one of the speakers and talk about creating an extraordinary life and how to get funding for your company and build new deals. I asked Tony Robbins to hold the elevator as he and his team were running to get on it. And then I said, "There's a very good friend of yours that would like to say hello. As a matter of fact, there are a couple of other folks that would love to say hello too." I introduced them all; I never talked about me. After his good friend came down and gave him a hug and got reconnected with him, Tony looked at me and said, "Hey, what is your name, and what do you do?" I told him my name and explained that I run a venture capital and business coaching firm, helping companies all over the country launch and grow their businesses. He asked me how I did that, and I said, "Consistently." I also shared that I was a big fan and anytime he needed help in filling his events, I would be honored to help. Since that time I have been honored to share the stage with him and learn from his expertise.

I also had a desire to connect with Mark Victor Hansen, co-author of *Chicken Soup for the Soul*. I tried several times to network with him and failed miserably each time. I finally had the chance to help him with a book launch when his book tour was coming to Chicago. Within three days we created a power lunch for his roadshow with almost 300 people, and I helped him sell more books at our power lunch than at all of his other stops in Chicago. I could have said no to the lunch and missed the opportunity. When Mark walked in, the place it was totally packed. He said to me, "I am not sure who you are or how you did this, but you and I are going to do a lot of business together." A decade later we are still great friends and work on events and projects all over the world!

Now is the time to elevate your game when it comes to building great connections. Now is the time to make the choice to surround yourself with champions on a regular basis! A special thanks to Craig Duswalt for launching this book and his 100 percent dedication to helping others succeed!

Bill Walsh is the CEO and founder of the business coaching/venture capital firm Powerteam International. Bill hosts and speaks at events all over the world, and his passion is empowering entrepreneurs and business owners to create massive success. He loves to help people to understand specifically what it takes to build successful companies. He is an accomplished author, speaker, radio personality, and movie celebrity. He has a very successful background in finance and marketing and has spent two decades working with start-ups to major global brands to increase sales, productivity, and overall success. He is an innovator with a remarkable ability to determine and dictate success strategy to seize global market opportunities.

www.BillWalsh360.com

THREE SECRETS TO BEING
AN AMAZING SPEAKER

Joel Weldon

Imagine that you're so shy and lacking in confidence that in four years of high school you never once gave an oral report. Speaking in front of others was impossible for you. Public speaking wasn't a skill you possessed, and it wasn't something you even wanted to learn how to do.

How then do you explain that, at age thirty-three, you became one of three finalists in the Toastmasters International Speech Contest, competing in front of over two thousand people? Then, just ten years later, at age forty-three, you're inducted into the Professional Speakers Hall of Fame and earn over a million dollars that year as a professional speaker. Add that for the past forty-four years you were paid to speak at events all over the world, over three thousand times, and you personally coached or critiqued well over ten thousand other speakers.

This is actually the true life story of Joel Weldon. In this chapter he'll share with you the three things he discovered about being an effective speaker and communicator. Today he is recognized as one of the best speakers and speaking skills coaches in the world.

I know this to be true. I've seen it with my own eyes! My name is Judy Weldon, Joel's wife of fifty-four years. Joel and I met at Sunday School when we were fifteen and seventeen, and we've been together ever since.

Now it's your turn to take your speaking skills to a higher level so you can grow your business by using the three discoveries my life partner has used himself, and taught to thousands of others. Get set for some great ideas!

Thank you, Judy! And readers, you'll be glad you're still reading this chapter about becoming a RockStar in your business and growing your business by being an even better speaker. Imagine feeling relaxed, confident, and connected to your audience every time you speak. It's not only possible—it's the direct result of doing just three things that I discovered years ago about speaking.

#1 – It's All About Your Audience and Their NFVs

That's right, it's not about you, so you need to find out as much about your audience as possible, such as the ratio of men to women, their age, experience level, knowledge of your subject, etc. NFV stands for Needs, Fears, and Victories. Most speakers don't even think about the NFVs of their audience!

Imagine how connected you'd be if you knew exactly what your audience needed to be doing that they're not doing now. Then you found out through questions and pre-event interviews what their fears were—things like worries, concerns, and what keeps them up at night. The victories are your audience's successes, achievements, claim to fame.

That's what my first two questions were to Craig Duswalt when he asked me to write this chapter for you. 1) Who is this aimed at? and 2) What are their NFVs?

Let's see if Craig and I are on target. You're an entrepreneur, author, speaker, or business owner. You need practical ideas to help you move forward even faster. You need specifics that can produce immediate results for you, and will give you a big financial return and a RockStar image. Is that on target?

You're also concerned that there are so many different ideas out there that you get frustrated with too many things to do. Some of your friends and acquaintances are moving faster than you, and you wonder, *When will I skyrocket ahead?* As far as speaking goes, you're good, maybe even very good. Yet you've seen other speakers make offers from the stage and generate huge results, far beyond what you're getting. You wonder, *What do they know that I don't know, and how do I get that good?* Do any of those concerns connect with you?

As far as victories go, I know these are right on target. You are motivated, you're willing to work and put forth the energy to succeed at an even higher level. How do I know that is you? You're still reading this! That fact alone puts you automatically in the top 5 percent. Congratulations!

Imagine how much more confident you'd feel, how much more of a connection you'd have with your audience, if you only talked about things that met their needs! Helped them overcome a fear! Reinforced a victory or success! You'd be a RockStar in your audience's eyes. Your business would grow, and you'd be positioning yourself as a RockStar expert.

Now find out their NFVs and create your message around your Golden Thread!

#2 – Your Golden Thread

Before you even begin thinking about your specific content—stories, statistics, examples, analogies—create one sentence that sums up your entire message.

This chapter contains this Golden Thread: "Use speaking to grow your business and position yourself as a RockStar expert by using three powerful speaking tools."

Yes, you read about my personal story, the audience and their NFVs, and now the Golden Thread. All that is focused on helping you become an even better speaker.

Now, what's your Golden Thread going to be? Once you have it crystal clear in your mind, you'll know exactly what you can and cannot put into your message.

Your content should focus specifically on ideas that meet a need, overcome a fear, or reinforce a victory, and be 100 percent connected to each audience. The Golden Thread gives you that ability.

#3 – Your Call to Action

Since your objective is to grow your business through speaking, you've got to create action. Without action by your audience, your message hasn't accomplished anything. For example, "Think about what it means to be free! Feel a renewed sense of gratitude for the good in your life!"

The most beneficial type of Call to Action is the one that asks for doable action! When your audience hears your Doable Call to Action, they think, *I can do that, and I will do that!*

If selling your book is the Call to Action, what if you said: "My book regularly sells for $24.95. You can get it today for only $20. Then just read pages twenty-three to twenty-seven. If you haven't earned at least five times your $20 with those ideas, send the book back, and you'll get a full refund!"

When you speak next . . .

Know your audience's NFVs.

Focus on your Golden Thread.

Make your Call to Action DOABLE!

––––––––––

Joel Weldon is a founding member of the National Speakers Association, has been inducted into the Speakers Hall of Fame, and has received the Golden Gavel Award. His Ultimate Speaking System has been used by thousands of speakers, authors, and business owners. Joel can be contacted directly at joelweldonspeaker@gmail.com, or you can reach him by phone at 1-800-852-8572. (That is, if he's not out on his private, competitive, slalom waterski lake in Arizona!)

www.SuccessComesInCans.com

ROCKSTAR BARBECUE: HOW I TURNED MY BACKYARD GRILL INTO A $500 MILLION RESTAURANT EMPIRE

"Famous Dave" Anderson, America's Rib King

When Craig Duswalt reached out to me for a RockStar story about my life for his upcoming new book, I first thought, *I'm no Rock-Star; I'm just a cook!* But after thinking about the character traits of a RockStar, I realized there's a lot to my life that is very similar to a RockStar. Most RockStars live the first half of their life in relative obscurity and near poverty, spending countless hours daily perfecting their craft until that magical moment when one of their songs becomes a hit, and overnight they become RockStars. Generally, substance abuse fuels this trajectory until they crash and burn, and if they're lucky, they get sober and continue to rock on to the delight of their raving loyal fans. *OK,* I thought, *my own life in many ways really* is *like that of a RockStar.*

I have spent the first half of my life driven to make great, award-winning, tasty, juicy, mouthwatering barbecued ribs. Once people tasted my barbecue, they demanded that I open restaurants in their cities, and grocery stores couldn't keep enough of my award-winning barbecue sauces stocked on their shelves. I too had my moments of near death, bankruptcy, and substance abuse. Fortunately I turned my life around, and I'm alive today to tell this "from humble beginnings" story of how I turned my backyard grill into a $500 million restaurant empire!

My story is one of hope and inspiration. If I could succeed, then anyone can succeed. I wasn't born with rich parents. I wasn't the smartest kid in class. I wasn't particularly gifted—but the one thing I had was a dream, a passion for great-tasting ribs, and a willingness to work harder than anyone else that drove me nonstop until I succeeded at becoming America's Rib King—last year selling over 16 million pounds of ribs!

In thinking about what I could share that would be meaningful and inspiring, I immediately knew this wasn't going to be a story where I would spill the beans about what was in the secret sauce. I realized I needed to share the street-smart strategies that could change a life or help jump-start someone's career. These life lessons are never taught in school; the only way I could have discovered them was through my own toughest challenges and adversities.

A lot of people say, "Dave, it would be so cool just to be in your shoes—everything you touch seems to turn to gold!" I quickly reply to them, "You have no idea what you are asking! I don't think you want to be as broke as I have been. I don't think you want to work the hours I work day in and day out, month after month, year after year, without taking vacations—or even wanting to take a vacation. And I seriously don't think you want to deal with life's most difficult problems and the crushing adversities I have dealt with."

If you take anything away from what I share with you, it's that anything is possible, but more importantly, you can't live your life only focused on accomplishing your own dreams. This is key: If you live your life with an obsessive devotion to making "other people's lives" more meaningful, happier, and more abundant, these people will make sure that you are able to realize your life's wildest dreams. I was frustrated when I was living my life just for myself. Tough lesson to learn that it's not about me, but it's all about putting the other person first.

First, you need to know that my first business loan in 1973 was for $10,000, and I got this money from a bank without any collateral or cosigners, and this is pretty significant because $10,000 was a whole lot of money at that time. My whole life has been filled with examples of "How in the world did you ever pull that one off—it's just not possible!" Even though I was in the bottom half of the class in high school and I don't have an undergraduate degree, I received my master's degree from Harvard University and had everything—my tuition, room and board—all paid for! I have a White House Presidential Appointment, and I served as Assistant Secretary in the US Department of the Interior. My Famous Dave's restaurants have been recognized by my peers and the National Restaurant Association as one of "America's Hottest Concepts," and the National Barbecue Association has declared that my new barbecue restaurant, Jimmie's Old Southern, as one of the "Best in America"!

I have been inducted into the National Entrepreneur's Hall of Fame, and in 2017 I was inducted into the American Royal Barbecue Hall of Fame. I have received Oprah Winfrey's Angel Award for a lifetime of work with at-risk Native American Youth. I have appeared on the Food Network, Discovery Channel, Travel Channel, PBS, CBS, ABC, NBC, WGN, and over 500 radio stations. Yes, you could say that this kid who grew up on the streets of Chicago has achieved RockStar status.

So, what is the difference between what I do and others who struggle every day to make ends meet and live frustrated lives?

I believe that my life changed the moment I understood "it's not about me!"—which is really a strange statement for a RockStar. I learned that if I could make other people outrageously happy, I would be able to create raving loyal fans—almost as though they were addicted to me. In my mind, they needed me. They couldn't do without me. The loved my ribs! My passion in life has always been making the best barbecue possible. My award-winning ribs are mouthwatering, tender, juicy, and tasty! And when I char them over smoldering embers and caramelize my Best in America BBQ Sauce on these ribs—Good Lorda' Mercy—they *are* addicting!

Strive to be the best you can be for the purposes of making others delightfully happy, and soon these people will be your adoring fans. When you are obsessive devoted to making other people happy, they will be obsessively devoted to you—and you will soon be living the RockStar life!

Dave Anderson is America's Rib King, best known as "Famous Dave," the founder of Famous Dave's of America with over 150 restaurants, $400 million in sales, and nearly 800 Best of Class awards. Dave has helped found several publicly traded companies on Wall Street, creating over 20,000 new jobs and billions in sales. Dave's amazing "against all odds" life story can be best described as "The Man Who Won't Quit!" having experienced adversity, frustration, and bankruptcy as well as tremendous success. Throughout his success Dave has always believed that his higher purpose in life is to make a positive difference in the lives of others.

americasribking@gmail.com

chaotic circumstances. No matter the level of discomfort at the time, when dealing with family and friends, I tried to be as cool and positive as possible with a smile. Even my first comments under medical duress were usually in the fashion of Apollo 13 astronaut, Jim Lovell, who calmly exclaimed in crisis, "Houston, we have a problem." Now that's Tone!

Tenacity: I agree with Thomas Edison: Genius is 1 percent inspiration and 99 percent perspiration. There's no substitute for hard work in understanding all aspects of an issue, being involved and visible to teammates, setting standards, and applying sustained effort to strive for a solution. The most tenacious leaders I've seen in the military placed the burden of overcoming the most difficult circumstances on their own backs ahead of their personal comfort and ambition. Succinctly, they just tried harder, and they demonstrated an indomitable spirit while serving our nation. Pick any Medal of Honor awardee from any conflict, and I'll guarantee the one characteristic they have in common is Tenacity.

To sum it up, I consistently relied upon the inspirational framework of "Teamwork, Tone, Tenacity" to overcome the Unexpected, Unwanted, and Uncertainty and triumph over cancer. I am now, thank God, two years into a stable remission. MM is still an incurable malignancy, but it is treatable, and my way ahead is regular low-dose maintenance chemotherapy treatments. Considering all the potential outcomes, this is a great place to be. I hope my actions in this personal crisis serve as an example to others that "Teamwork, Tone, Tenacity" can be applied against any type of adversity, especially when the stakes are extremely high. Teamwork, Tone, Tenacity: They rocked my life and are allowing me to help others . . . and that is truly the best revenge against cancer!

Rear Admiral Paul Becker, USN (Ret.), is a highly decorated veteran who served around the globe in peace, crisis, and combat as a Naval Intelligence Officer. Upon retirement in 2016, he founded The Becker T3 Group LLC, a consultancy focused on improving organizations' bottom line by applying leadership's core tenets of "Teamwork, Tone, Tenacity." He is a dynamic keynote speaker whose articles and interviews have been widely published. A Stage IV Bone Marrow cancer survivor, he regularly inspires health care professional and patient audiences by sharing firsthand lessons for overcoming adversity.

paul83becker@gmail.com

VALUES AND PERSISTENCE

Gary Howarth

At the age of thirty-nine, I was your typical Type A industrial sales rep. I was traveling all over the world selling materials to the memory disk and aerospace industries. Being on the road over 60 percent of the time, I seldom spent a lot of time with my family and friends. When I was home, I would be working all the time at all hours of the day and night, communicating with clients both in Asia and Europe. I enjoyed it, but I was also very self-centered.

That Christmas, my wife, Terri, and I took a trip to visit friends in Oregon. While at my friend's home in Central Oregon, Roger and I were in his backyard chopping firewood for the night. I felt awful when we were finished. After I rested for an hour, I began to feel better. Terri insisted that I see the doctor when we got home to figure out what was wrong. I thought I was just a little overweight and out of shape, but I reluctantly agreed to go after a long discussion.

After my check-up that included EKGs, echocardiograms, CAT scans, X-rays, and MRIs, the doctors concluded that I needed to have surgery to remove my pericardium because it had calcified and was squeezing my heart so it could not function properly. I almost died and would have within weeks had it not been discovered in time. God needed to hit me with this two-by-four to get my attention.

The surgery was successful, and after a few months I was good as new. Coming so close to dying really opened my eyes to what was important. I decided to spend more time with my wife and not take work so seriously. Eventually I left my international selling position and decided to work as a manufacturer's sales rep. I became my own boss. I worked for four different companies selling a variety of products and was able to keep some of my long-term domestic customers.

I was much happier. Spending more time with Terri and doing more personal traveling was rewarding, and it improved our relationship. I was able to control my own schedule and work when I wanted. I did this for a few years and was enjoying life and my new freedom. As time went on, however, I started to work more and more and fall back into the same old routine I had several years before. Then my world turned upside down again. I believe that God needed to hit me upside the head with a two-by-four again to get my attention about what is important in life.

In the cold winter of 2010, Terri was diagnosed with Stage 4 uterine cancer. By the time it was discovered, it had already spread to her lymph nodes. I was grateful for having my manufacturer's rep business, because it allowed me to become her full-time caretaker. This new event served to remind me about what is the most valuable thing in life. It is the relationships we have, and we should never, never, never take them for granted.

For the next two years, Terri was in and out of the hospital, undergoing several surgeries and multiple treatments to slow the growth of the cancer. During that time, I was by her side almost all the time and did whatever needed to be done. We also became much closer, and it truly cemented our love for each other. Being fully present and in the moment was a huge gift I received through this experience.

After two years of fighting her cancer, she passed away at home in my arms.

At this point, I was lost. For the last two years, I had taken on the role of caretaker. In an instant, I was no longer a caretaker. I hadn't worked much during the last two years, so I wasn't a working person either. I had nothing from the outside that defined who I was. Now I was lost, searching for a new meaning in my life.

A couple months later, I was sitting next to my nephew Ryan at a family function at the Elks Lodge in Moreno Valley. He told me he had an idea for a new business. At this point, I was open to anything and asked him to share his ideas with me. Ryan came up with the idea of a musical video greeting card. I thought it was a fantastic idea, and we started to develop the business.

I loved the idea, because it was all about connecting and growing relationships in a fun and entertaining way. It also provided a project for me that fulfilled what was important to me. I know Terri would have loved it.

We developed the concept and hired a programmer. The entire process was and is quite a learning experience. The first iteration was Sing Your Card. It was a lot of fun. It provided a way for people to create their own video greeting card with custom music written by Ryan. However, the majority of people were physically repulsed by the thought that they needed to sing in order to use the service. We needed to make a change.

We reconfigured the program and changed the name to Record It Cards. This removed the idea that people had to sing, and it was much better received by the market. Two years later, though, it still wasn't taking off. Time for another revision.

What we then developed was a video messaging service. We changed the name to VaxisHub. We added features that would be beneficial to entrepreneurs and businesses that rely on developing strong personal relationships with their clients while standing out from the crowd by doing something that other competitors weren't doing. Right now we are focusing on the insurance industry and have added animated explainer video libraries that explain different products in a fun and entertaining way. It is being very well received.

It has been five years since Ryan and I first discussed being in business together at the Elks Lodge. Persistence in keeping with the concept, listening to the market, and sticking to our values of creating a place where people can connect and develop personal relationships has resulted in a successful business that would make Terri proud.

———————

Gary Howarth sold technical products for over thirty years with several international organizations, including Union Carbide, Praxair, Baikowski International, and AIM MRO. He was responsible for sales in North America, Asia, Europe, and South America. In addition to technical sales, Gary is a serial entrepreneur. His most recent venture is a video messaging service called VaxisHub. VaxisHub.com provides a platform for sending professional video emails for that personal touch with prospects and clients.

Gary served as chairman of the La Verne Chamber of Commerce. He also serves on the board of directors for the Rose City Counseling Center in Pasadena.

www.VaxisHub.com

I WAS THE ROCK IN THE MIDDLE OF THE RIVER

Chris Kopf

My wife, Francene, said: "I want a divorce . . ." We had three daughters, ages five, six, and seven, and they were full of laughter, fun, ballet, soccer, dolls, and scraped knees.

We had a big, beautiful house, a maid, a country club membership, a second home in the mountains, luxury vacations . . . life was great!

I had worked my butt off for twenty years to succeed in sales and sales management in the highly competitive technology industry. I was a top executive and a part of the inner-circle at a two-billion-dollar Silicon Valley company. I had a hefty income and millions of dollars' worth of stock options.

I had just been promoted to run a new worldwide OEM relationship with Hitachi. This was a big job, and a huge stepping-stone for me and my career.

I had a flight to London on Sunday for a weeklong trip to kick off the partnership, and every other major city in the US and the world were on my calendar.

Prior to my trip, Francene had something she wanted to tell me, and other things she did not. After hours of tears, shouting, arguing, and mostly unanswered questions, she said: "I want a divorce." I was devastated, hurt, resentful, and angry.

Francene had changed. I could see she was struggling. My absence created gaps that she filled with drinking, marathon training, shopping, and other escapes that were exciting to her.

She needed help. *We* needed help. I realized that I had become a part-time husband and father, and the value of millions of dollars in the bank and all the material things were worthless if I lost my wife and we broke up our family.

The next morning, I went into work—and I quit my job.

I told Francene that I was not going anywhere. Despite her feelings and actions, I was 100 percent focused on helping her, supporting her, and saving our marriage and our family.

I became "Mr. Mom." I made all the meals, drove our daughters to and from school, their play dates, and all their activities.

Francene went through the motions as we met with our minister, a marriage counselor, and individual psychologists. After a couple of months, she was tired of talking about herself, her feelings, and us. She was reluctant to change, and she was tired of being a wife and a mother.

I met individually with our marriage counselor, and he agreed that he saw no progress. He said he was sorry, but it was very unlikely we would save our marriage.

We continued to meet twice per week with our marriage counselor, and during one of our sessions he recommended that Francene attend an Alcoholics Anonymous meeting.

She was in denial but agreed to go to an AA meeting. She thought she would learn how to drink responsibly. . . . Instead they convinced her to quit drinking and commit to ninety meetings in ninety days. In support, I stopped drinking alcohol as well and began to attend Al-Anon meetings. This was a turning point in her recovery and our marriage. The wisdom in these meetings and the 12-step program changed both of our perspectives—and saved our marriage.

Almost a year after those fateful words, "I want a divorce," we met in a small chapel at our church. With our minister and our three young daughters present, we renewed our vows and exchanged crosses.

I decided to design my new career as an entrepreneur with limited travel, leveraging my background and skill set.

A great friend and I created a company called LightPoint Impressions: We built and bought billboards in Texas, Oklahoma, Indiana, and South Carolina. I had invested the majority of the money to fund this company, and by 2009 we had created a solid inventory of assets and a recurring income stream that we were reinvesting into the company.

I was able to be home to attend all the parent-teacher conferences, the ballet recitals, and the school plays. I became Chief in my daughter's Indian Princess tribes, and I was the soccer coach for my youngest daughter's team. I even joined the elementary PTA as the first dad to become an officer, and I co-chaired the annual fund-raising auction.

After about six years with dwindling funds, Francene and I decided to sell our large home in Dallas and move into our vacation home in the small ski resort town of Crested Butte, Colorado.

In May of 2009 I reinvented myself once again and got my real estate license. Not exactly great timing, as there were very few people buying vacation homes in the mountains—this was the midst of the recession, the Wall Street meltdown, and the real estate crash.

Within three years of my first sale, I climbed into the top ten of the 175 real estate agents in my market. The next year I was the number one agent in my market and among the top 2 percent of the 87,000 Coldwell Banker real estate agents worldwide. I continue to be one of the top agents in my market and the world, consistently earning over a half million dollars annually.

I have also become a speaker, author, and coach to help other agents leverage the systems I have put in place to become a RockStar in my market.

Best of all, I have been present as a husband and father. Francene is an awesome mom, a beautiful wife, and my best friend. Our marriage is strong. Our daughters are doing great, with two attending the University of Colorado; our oldest graduated a year ago and is working in Denver, successfully selling advertising for a magazine.

The difficult sacrifices and changes we made paid off. I chose to not give in or give up. I was determined to be the rock in the middle of the river for my wife and family and fight the current that was threatening to wash our marriage and family away. I am thankful for the journey—physically, mentally, and spiritually.

Chris Kopf is a top real estate agent in the resort town of Crested Butte, Colorado. He is a professional speaker, author, coach, and the creator of The Resort Real Estate Agent System for Success—How to Become a Top Real Estate Agent in Your Resort Market. Chris teaches quick and easy tips to help agents transform their real estate business—and their life!

www.ResortRealEstateCoach.com

HOW I LET GO OF A LIFETIME FEAR AROUND MONEY

Chris McLean, MA

I got my first job at fourteen, and I've worked hard ever since. Along the way, plenty of people were willing to teach me how to work, but I never asked, "What's the right way to keep and spend the money I've earned?"

Without that knowledge, I lived my entire adult life spending every dollar I made . . . carrying credit card debt . . . living paycheck to paycheck . . . and constantly allowing my "net worth" to determine my "self-worth" (both ending up in a "negative balance" on a regular basis).

Things slowly got worse, and yet I still refused to ask for help. As a result, debt took me places I never wanted to go, kept me longer than I wanted to stay, and cost me more than I ever thought I'd pay.

I finally enrolled in my first budgeting course, which gave me lots of information but did little to change my existing money habits and beliefs. The budgeting message was "just stop doing what you've been doing for a lifetime and start doing these other things today!" It's kind of like going to the doctor's office where they tell you to "just quit smoking" or "just lose weight." That's good information, but knowing it doesn't always change one's behavior. That budgeting course didn't work for me because it felt like a "crash diet approach" to spending money, and most studies prove crash diets just don't work!

Still, I kept searching and eventually spoke with two different people who were debt-free and at peace with their finances. They both asked me the same question: "Where does your money go each month?"

I told them, "I have no idea," to which they both replied, "THAT is your problem!"

They then suggested a simple method for "tracking my spending, a few minutes every day, for the next thirty days." "And then," they continued, "after thirty days, total it up, and look at the results. Once you see your spending habits and know where the money is actually going, you're bound to make better financial choices."

"Just try it," they said, "and over time, these small steps will turn your entire life around."

Having nothing to lose, I tried their "baby step approach" and in only thirty days saw (for the first time) how much money I spent on unimportant things, I didn't spend enough on the things that mattered, and I was under-earning by almost $1,000 dollars per month!

Even though I didn't like what thirty days of those numbers told me, I actually felt a glimmer of hope that I would one day gain control of my money. I felt empowered.

I started that practice in May of 2007, and I have faithfully continued reviewing my numbers every month since then. As a result, I went from owing $100,000 in credit card debt and owning a condo I couldn't afford to:

- living debt-free for the past nine years
- building a six-month cash reserve for emergencies
- saving an additional $30,000 in cash for my next used-car purchase by paying myself a monthly car payment
- investing in an IRA that I actually understand
- and most importantly, feeling a sense of confidence, self-esteem, and pride with money that I had never known before

Now if you're wondering what "magic" changed me from a lifetime debtor into a responsible adult with money, let me break it down for you:

Our brains are designed to learn habits through repetitive behavior. Once those habits are learned, they're locked into a part of the brain called the basal ganglia. It's a scientific fact that you cannot "break" a habit stored in the basal ganglia for it will always be a part of you.

Unfortunately, budget courses ask people to break every lifelong habit we've ever created around money, and the brain simply doesn't work like that! Willpower alone never beats the power of habit, and that's why so few people stick to their budgets!

The human brain is a habit-learning machine. We learn new habits every day because the brain is designed to quickly learn new and simple tasks with ease.

Tracking my spending for three minutes a day didn't ask me to break my spending habits. It gave me a very simple, new habit to learn (which the brain loves to do!).

Once I saw the pattern of my spending, I made different, CONSCIOUS choices with money instead of falling back on my UNCONSCIOUS habits.

I then began reading books on the psychology of money, which led me to enroll in a psychology master's degree program. I focused my studies on "how can I work WITH the brain to help people get out of debt, stay out of debt, and build personal wealth?"

The result? After graduating in 2015, I created "The Abundant Life Game," which is a simple, thirty-day money game played in teams of four designed to help individuals, couples, and the self-employed learn healthy financial habits in a fun, safe, and supportive environment. All research shows that when you teach topics using a game format, learning is greatly accelerated. I've taught this simple game to over a thousand people at my two-day workshops so they'll never have to go through the same financial fear I went through for most of my life.

Looking back, my greatest accomplishments around money are not measured externally by the balance in my savings account, but rather by my inner sense of peace, clarity, and confidence. I know that no matter what happens, I'll be OK.

My other accomplishment was the courage and willingness to break my isolation and ask for help, even when that search led me to dead ends. I just kept going, and to me, that's a true sign of inner courage.

No matter where you are in your relationship with money, I encourage you to reach out, stretch, and continue moving forward toward the abundant life God intends for all of us to live.

Chris McLean, MA, helps individuals, families, and self-employed business owners overcome their fear and confusion surrounding personal finance. Chris' engaging personality and ability to explain money concepts in a very simple way has helped thousands of people gain financial clarity, get out of debt, and live better lives. He's the author of the award-winning books *Financial Wisdom* and *Why Budgets Don't Work!*

Chris' signature two-day workshop, "The Abundant Life Game," teaches people how to play a fun, thirty-day money game that builds healthy financial habits in a safe and supportive environment.

www.MoneyCoachChris.com

NEVER, EVER GIVE UP

Scott Zimmerman

I started out in the financial services industry at the age of twenty-two back in 1989. I was attending college, getting ready to graduate, and had already purchased a small life insurance policy from a friend of mine who was a life insurance agent. I was trying to find my way in the business world, so after purchasing a small IRA from him, he recommended that I talk to his father, the agency manager. His father interviewed me and offered me a position within their agency. It was commission only; they offered jobs to everyone. My friend was very successful and took me under his wing, teaching me everything he knew.

The first few years were very difficult, to say the least. My dad was a contractor, and my mother a payroll specialist. I didn't have much to fall back on, in the event I didn't succeed, other than the fact that my parents didn't charge me rent.

In the beginning, I made cold calls out of the phone book, called every family member I had, and talked to everyone I encountered about life insurance. Times were tough as a twenty-two-year-old trying to sell insurance, pay my bills, and survive. I persisted for about three years and was failing miserably. I remember every Sunday looking in the paper for jobs to apply for. I loved what I was doing, but I was miserable inside, trying to get people to buy insurance from me. I did have some successes here and there, and that's what kept me in the game!

When I was twenty-three, I moved into a horrible apartment with my friend. My rent was $297 per month, and I was late every month! I wasn't making it, so I just kept my head down, networked, tried to stay positive, and kept moving forward. From the age of twenty-three to twenty-five, while trying to make a career out of being a life insurance professional, I found ways to supplement my earnings. By delivering pizzas two nights a week, and by helping a friend who owned a janitorial company two other nights out of the week, I barely got by. I used this money to help pay for marketing and to help me cultivate relationships with CPAs by taking them out to lunch and coffee. I got married at the age of twenty-five and was just trying to keep everything afloat. Finally, after many years of persisting, working hard, and staying focused, my business began to flourish.

I attribute my success to many things: my positive attitude, my determination to help people, my drive to become successful, and having a no-quit attitude. In this way I was able to see the light and figure out how to succeed in my business.

It's been twenty-eight years, and I have been very fortunate to help thousands of people plan for the "what ifs" in life. What happens if . . . someone were to die prematurely, someone doesn't live to their full life expectancy and they're taking care of their loved ones, someone becomes sick or hurt and is unable to work, someone needs care in their home or nursing home, someone is planning to retire and they need to ensure they have enough income for them and their spouse . . .

My firm specializes in life insurance, disability insurance, long-term care insurance, safe money investments, health insurance, and employee benefits.

The services we provide help people take care of themselves and the ones they love—their spouses, partners, children, grandchildren, business partners, charities, and employees.

David, one of my favorite clients, was a super nice guy who owned a very successful pharmacy. His CPA referred him to me. When we first met, he asked me to help him with his employee benefit plan. A couple of years later he bought life insurance to protect his wife if something happened to him. A few years later David also bought long-term care insurance for himself and his wife. After a few years, David discovered that his investment advisor was taking advantage of him, so we moved several million dollars over to some safe money investments. David and I became fairly close friends. This wasn't just about him buying insurance from me. I always strive to have a relationship with all of my clients.

Fast-forward to about three years ago. He came down with dementia and started forgetting things; he was having problems. It started very slowly. His wife called me and informed me that they had to sell their business immediately because he was declining quickly. We had to use the long-term care insurance to bring them help at home. We started using income from their investments to live on, since they sold the business and their income had ceased, and we met with their lawyer to make sure their life insurance was set up correctly.

When I met Dave, he was really with it—a great husband, father, grandfather, and business owner. Over a twenty-year period, his whole life had changed. Luckily, Dave structured all of the right planning for himself and his family. As a result, they were all well taken care of.

Most people tell me that they wish they would have planned better and taken the extra time to ensure they had the proper coverage. Many people seem to live for today and put off the planning that is so essential. This is my goal: to help people gain peace of mind, knowing that they too will be OK in the event of a "what if."

What I've realized in my life and career is that you must focus on doing the right things for people and never give up. Be honest, positive, grateful, focused, and have integrity. This is the formula to accomplishing just about anything you want in life.

Scott Zimmerman helps his clients strategize properly for their financial future to ensure that they have fail-safe planning in place to maximize their peace of mind. He makes certain that their investments are in the right products so they're never exposed to the risk of running out of money. Scott establishes a secure plan in which his clients have the ultimate protection and coverage necessary for themselves, their spouses, and their loved ones. Helping clients achieve "peace of mind" is Scott's goal. Scott has been a trusted advisor, speaker, and author within the financial services industry since 1989, and he is partner in a financial services firm in Los Angeles, California. In addition, he is the co-creator of the Life Insurance Audit, The Annuity Audit, The 21st Century HR Solution, and the Perfect LTC Solution.

www.Corpstrat.com
www.SafeMoneyScott.com

HOW A SHY CHOIR GIRL WENT FROM SINGING ON SUNDAYS TO ROCKING STAGES AROUND THE WORLD

Tesy Ward

Music has always been a driving force in my life, as far back as I can remember. My earliest memories are a blissful mix of traditional Irish tunes peppered with R&B, rock 'n' roll, and American standards. Being a woman of faith, singing in a variety of choirs was not merely a hobby but a cultural rite. Throughout good times and bad, no matter what the circumstance, there was always the music. It was a force which became my solace, my companion, and my soul.

As the years passed, and my life began to take shape, becoming gently molded by a rich education and a mélange of experiences, a poignant question emerged: "Where would music fit in?" I was not enrolled in a collegiate music study program, so would music have to fall by the wayside, in favor of more traditional entrepreneurial ventures? I was now facing a life-altering fork in the road—of a magnitude so great, it shook me to my very core.

As a bevy of thoughts and possibilities swirled about in my young head, one became abundantly clear: Music is my dominant life force, and without it, I might as well die. The question now became, "How do I financially support myself while living my dream, my passion, my music?" Well, it has taken a lifetime to compile the secrets and tips I'm about to share, but whether your dream is to become a RockStar or a RockStar Entrepreneur, here are the steps I feel will help you on your journey.

Your Plan

Stardom, fame, and monetary success—those elusive, much-sought-after goals—are supposed to be the fruits of arduous labor. If the aforementioned is true, then why do so many rock stars and entrepreneurs fall short of grabbing, and more significantly, *retaining* the brass ring of success? While each case is different, the blame usually rests squarely on the lack of planning and the in-

51

ability to execute said plan. Join me as we examine a few of the crucial steps in turning your dreams into a profitable reality.

Hire a Band

In music, the end product is a synergistic compilation of melodies and lyrics which convey a theme. Musicians, each precisely playing a different instrument, join forces and combine efforts to produce a musical piece whose sum is far greater than its individual parts. The same holds true for business. Assembling a worthy team, one whose talents and goals are closely aligned, is crucial to the success of any business. In the early stages, it's important to stress quality over quantity. Having an excessive, ineffective team is the quickest way to ensure failure as opposed to success. A cohesive, motivated, and focused team is the hallmark of any successful venture. Keeping your team engaged, compensated, and anxious to reach the next milestone, is a recipe for lasting and meaningful success.

Play Gigs

Simply put, this translates into "get out there and do what you do best!" If you're a lead singer, sing to whomever will listen. If your dream is to become a motivational speaker, get on a stage and deliver your message! Contrary to popular opinion, no one becomes a rock star overnight. Dreams are a catalyst, but true success lies in the mastery of your craft.

Choose Your "Target Audience"—Not a Record Label

There is rarely a musician I meet, who upon learning that I develop, represent, and manage talent, does not ask me to secure them a record label contract with an accompanying large signing bonus. Unfortunately, their thoughts and visions are skewed, at best. There are no quick paychecks without demands and expectations attached. In today's world, the objective of musicians and entrepreneurs alike, should be geared towards securing a rabid fan base. The sparks of an existing, consistently loyal group of followers can be fanned into raging flames of success, through effectively identifying and meeting customers' needs and expectations, via innovative product offerings coupled with excellent service. Investors, lending institutions, and other key players, are far more inclined to support and nurture a venture that has already started to develop a track record as opposed to one that is still in the planning stages. Ah, but how does one accomplish this? Glad you asked—read on.

Social Media and All That Jazz

The goal of any effective social media program should be to get your message and/or product in front of as many people as possible so as to increase your following and convert fans into loyal, repeat customers. With today's ever changing array of platforms, social media can be your best friend or a source of angst and sheer terror.

Remembering a few key points can greatly increase your odds of success. Firstly, it's important to codify your brand—namely, who you are and what your corporate mission is. Offering a clear statement of what customers can expect from doing business with you goes a long way toward closing a sale and enjoying the benefits of a satisfied client. Secondly, it's not about what you like, but what your target audience wants and needs. Use social media to promote and expose yourself, but keep in mind it's a two-way street. Learn to not only listen to feedback, but actively seek it as well. Once feedback is received, it is best to take swift action to resolve problems and concerns. Loyal customers are the most valuable asset an entrepreneur possesses. Use their feedback to grow and enhance your business in a way which is mutually satisfying.

Staying on the Stage through Growth and Longevity

The sustainment and expansion of any entrepreneurial venture rests on the triad of customer identification, satisfaction, and retention. Entrepreneurs who map out a path to success, allowing for feedback, changes in customers' desires, and fluctuations in the marketplace are heads and shoulders above their competition. However, merely mapping out a plan will not insure success. True lasting success lies in the ability to break a plan into meaningful, manageable pieces, which can then be executed by a motivated and unified team. A steady crescendo towards growth, progress, and happy customers quickly changes a dream into a satisfying, profitable reality.

In closing, it's important to remember that not everyone can be in a band, and not all bands work out. The same is true in business. Choose your associates and goals wisely! Be mindful that all team members' contributions are not only complementary to your goal, but appropriately recognized. Group harmony and team synergy are difficult, but not impossible to achieve. It is important to remain focused, persistent, and dedicated to your goals. Above all else, persevere. Remember, RockStars don't quit and quitters don't rock!

———————————

Tesy Ward is a successful businesswoman and philanthropist, known for her ability to identify, cultivate, and bring to market "hidden gems" within the music and entertainment industries. Her unique approach to business emanates from a lifetime of experience as a singer, lyricist, and developer of musical talent.

www.TesyWard.com

WHAT'S IN YOUR BAG?

Miguel Sanchez

It was the summer of 1989. After several attempts, I finally convinced my mother to allow me to venture out away from home—to leave to pursue the American dream. Against her better judgment, she said yes. I left, and after two days on the bus, I finally arrived in Tijuana, Mexico, on the border between Mexico and California. I was sixteen years old.

I remember when I arrived, I saw a metal fence littered with wooden crosses. I asked, "What does that mean? What are those crosses for?" Someone said, "Those crosses signify all the people who died trying to reach the American Dream."

I pondered this, and at that moment, I committed to myself that my name would not be on one of those crosses. I wasn't going back defeated. I wasn't about to hang my dream on a metal fence.

I wouldn't give up! I tried the first time, and I failed. The second time, third, fourth—seventeen times I was told that I didn't belong, that this wasn't for me. On the eighteenth try, I made it across and landed in San Pedro, California.

My first source of income was collecting cans. San Pedro is a very beautiful town with a waterfront and many restaurants. I learned that I could collect cans, take them to the recycling center, and get paid. On the weekend thousands come to San Pedro. So I went through the trash digging for cans.

While collecting cans, I quickly learned how many it took to make a dollar. I started counting in my head: 97 cents, 99 cents, a dollar. As I put cans into my bag, I was counting. By the end of day I knew how much money I had. Monday morning I had several bags that I would load on my bicycle, go to the recycling center, and get cash.

You see, physically I was collecting cans. Symbolically, though, they were cans of possibilities. Yes, I can! Every time I put a can in my bag, it was another possibility. *Yes, I can* have the American Dream. *Yes, I can* have a brand-new car. *Yes, I can* make my dreams come true.

My question is: What's in your bag? What is possible in your life? Everything that's possible is already inside you. Most of us don't understand the final step after acquiring those possibilities. It doesn't help to run from conference to conference, read books, and study, if you never do anything with the information. It doesn't help to have all these abilities, but never manifest anything with them.

I live by the Four Ds of Success:

Dream

You must have a dream. You must have a vision of where you want to be in life.

My first dream was to eat a hamburger. My first hamburger came from a trash can! I ate a half-eaten hamburger while digging for cans. That doesn't mean that my dream didn't come true. It was part of it, so I continued. My vision was to have a nice house, a nice car, a nice family, and I got them all. But first you have to have a dream.

Determination

Determination! It doesn't matter how many times you get rejected. It doesn't matter how many times people tell you can't; no, it's not yours; no, you can't have it. Any obstacle that comes your way, destroy it!

The owner of one particular restaurant kicked me out because I was making a mess of his trash cans. He finally realized that I didn't understand what he was saying, so he got someone to translate. Eventually, the owner saw my persistence and determination. He said to him, "Ask him if he wants a job," to which I responded, "Yes, that's all I'm looking for. That's all I want. I want to work." So he said, "Clean the tables, keep the bathrooms clean, and take all the trash to the dumpsters." I said, "No problem, sir."

Within one year, I was managing that place. Today, twenty years later, I am partners with the people of these restaurants. DETERMINATION! It doesn't matter how many times they tell you that you can't have it! You have to be DETERMINED to get your DREAM.

Dedication

You must DEDICATE to what you want, day in and day out! I used to work eighteen to nineteen hours a day. I was the first one in, the last one out. They saw my DEDICATION. I was DEDICATED to this place. I am the first Hispanic to become part owners with these awesome people.

Discipline

DISCIPLINE is the glue that keeps everything together. DISCIPLINE kicks your butt every morning, saying, "You said you were going to do this—get up and do it!" DISCIPLINE is doing what you don't want to do, what is not comfortable, but you know that you must do it.

Dream. Determination. Dedication. Discipline.

I have a new program called Immigrants Making a Difference. Each month, we go to the Veterans Hospital in Long Beach, California, and feed the veterans for free. Here is a immigrant kid who once ate from the trash and is now feeding the masses. What is your dream?

You see, what I want you to understand is that I did not come to America to pursue the American Dream. Because when you are pursuing something, you are constantly chasing it, chasing it; you can't get it. I did not come to America to pursue the American Dream. I came to America to *experience* the American Dream. Most importantly, I came to America to *be* the American Dream.

What is it that you must conquer in your life? You have to remember that a dream is not something that you see as you go to sleep. A dream is something that doesn't let you go to sleep because you are constantly feeling it and constantly going after it.

Dreams don't come true. Plans do.

What is the plan for your life?

––––––––––––

Miguel Sanchez was born in Mexico City. He migrated to the United States at the age of sixteen. Due to his age and the language barrier, he couldn't find employment, so he began collecting cans in a tourist area of San Pedro, California.

His persistence eventually paid off, and he was offered a position as a dishwasher and janitor. With hard work, good ethics, and dedication, he became the restaurant manager at the age of eighteen. One year later he was promoted to general manager. Fast-forward twenty years, and Miguel now runs two very successful corporations.

www.MiguelSanchezSpeaker.com

HOW I PASSED THE MOST CRUCIAL TEST OF MY CAREER

Hepsharat Amadi, MD

I tell my children to always be open to learning, because you never know when the knowledge you attain might become crucial, or when Life will spring a test on you!

I am a conventionally trained family practice doctor who always understood that conventional medicine, while working well for emergencies, was not capable of helping an already healthy person become any healthier.

So I understood, before going to medical school, that my purpose in going there was just to lay the foundation for my medical knowledge, not to be the sum total of it. Little could I have imagined then that the extra knowledge I was on the path to acquiring would one day save my oldest child's eyesight and health.

My aspirations were higher than just managing illness by using drugs and surgery. I wanted to be able to help people get healthy and educated enough to minimize or eliminate their need for medication or emergency services.

That was why, a few years after graduating from SUNY at Stony Brook Medical School and completing my residency in Family Practice at Bronx-Lebanon Hospital, I began studying many different holistic health techniques, including earning my license in acupuncture and Chinese herbs at night and on weekends while continuing to work full-time at an outpatient clinic during the day.

My search for more knowledge about how to improve people's health naturally continued, and it was while I was attending yet another health-related seminar that I met a colleague who was also holistically oriented. He introduced me to the quantum biofeedback machine and that really changed my life.

Imagine a machine that consists of a laptop computer, to which a box is attached. The box has leads that can be plugged into it and attach to a patient's head, wrists and ankles, and act as transducers that detect the electromagnetic activity of the entire body. The most familiar analogies I can give you in conventional medicine are the EKG machine for the heart, or the EEG machine for monitoring brain waves.

tions for everyone. Who would I be if I didn't provide a budget for every single situation? It's not always the most expensive, but it's the best.

I take my most pride in my patient's success stories. For example, a wife thanked me for helping her husband and said, "I felt like I was on my honeymoon again. Thanks for saving our marriage." I put hearing aids on a baby at six months old and now that person is a vice president in an architectural firm. A man was about to lose his job, but instead he got promoted. I was able to help a mother who was in a severe depression and couldn't leave her house when previously she was very active. Her doctor was ready to diagnose her with dementia when I resolved her hearing issue. Now she can go to her Bible study group again and has even gotten a volunteer position in a nonprofit organization. The list goes on.

Nola Aronson began her working career as a special education teacher after graduating from the University of Hartford in 1975. After moving to Los Angeles, California, in 1978 and working with so many children that had speech and language problems, she decided to go to Cal State Long Beach for a master's degree in speech pathology. As part of the curriculum, she took a pediatric audiology course and found she could help people with a solution faster, and so she became an audiologist. At the same time, her love for business made her study that field, and she has trained many audiologists to become very successful on their own. She is the owner of Advanced Audiology, Santa Clarita's largest hearing diagnostics center.

www.scvadvancedaudiology.com

MY DREAMS, MY LIFE, MY MENTORS, MY WIFE

Paul Barbe

My Dreams

Have you ever looked at your world and wondered how you ended up where you are today? What were your dreams as a child? Are you living any of those dreams? When you look back at those childhood dreams, they could be anywhere from the time you were able to walk through high school. Our dreams and outlook on life constantly change during these early years of our lives.

Growing up, we all have dreams of being a firefighter, police officer, doctor, or lawyer. Some may also have dreams of playing professional sports. Whatever that dream may have been, were you focused enough to pursue the dream so you could accomplish what was necessary to live the dream?

I remember in the seventh grade deciding that I wanted to be an engineer. Specifically, I wanted to be an electrical engineer. However, as time passed I decided that my passion was more in the civil engineering career path.

My Life

Growing up, I had what could be considered a normal childhood. I played in the yard, rode my bike, and played with my friends.

I also remember taking piano lessons starting at the age of eight. The piano lessons lasted about a year, and then I decided that wasn't for me. I also tried various sports. I played one year of baseball, and I tried basketball when I was in the seventh grade and again when I was a freshman in high school. Neither of those were my forte because I was small in stature.

I did start playing golf when I was about ten years old. Again, I wasn't very good at it, but I really enjoyed playing. I was on the golf team and the swim team at various times during high school. But again, I was not very good at either.

Thinking back to my high school days, it occurred to me that I had lost focus of my desire to be an engineer. I struggled with some classes during high school. The one that sticks out the most is math. I barely passed algebra.

After high school I went to the local community college for one year and then quit. At that time, college was not for me. It wasn't until five years later that I went back to college with a new focus and drive to get my degree in engineering.

My Mentors

A *mentor* is defined as "someone who teaches or gives advice or guidance to someone less experienced." I have had many mentors in my life; I am sure we all have. All of our teachers in school and college are mentors. Our earliest mentors are our parents. You can also look to your friends, their parents, aunts, uncles, and many others who have shared anything from a tidbit of information to helping you complete a complex project.

All of these people have had an influence on where you are today. I challenge you to look back and try to remember those people in your life that influenced your chosen career, hobbies, or other likes.

My mentors were my parents, a good friend's parents, and a couple of my college professors. My parents taught me responsibility and to work hard. My friend's parents also taught me to work hard and gave encouragement to learn new skills. My college professors gave me insight into learning and what it really means.

My Wife

One of the most influential mentors in my life has been my wife, Gale. She has stood by me, encouraged me, and celebrated my successes. She was there for me while I was studying for my engineering exams. She always made me feel better when I would get the exam results to find out I hadn't passed. When I finally did pass my exams, she was just as happy as I was.

Knowing how I loved to golf, she found a golf pro to work with me. This pro and I became very good friends. And he did help me improve my game. However, I no longer play golf for reasons I cannot remember.

Once, while on a weekend getaway to Santa Barbara, I was watching sailboats coming into and going out of the Santa Barbara Marina. I made a comment to Gale that I always wanted to learn how to sail. She said without hesitation, "Go ahead." So here, all these years later, I love to sail, I race regularly, and I enjoy the occasional cruise to Catalina Island.

Take a look around: What were your dreams? What are your dreams now? Pick one and go after it. Think of how good you'll feel when you realize your dream. Life is a journey, and a short one at that. Too short to leave dreams sitting on a shelf gathering dust! Grab one, dust it off, and pursue it. Maybe find someone to share it with—you'll double the fun. You will learn new things and make new friends.

So don't chase your dreams—*live* your dreams. It may take time to fulfill that dream, but just think of the things you will learn, and the friends and mentors you will make along the way. This will add to your life's story. Then go share your story. That is the way you *rock your life*.

Paul Barbe is a brand-new author and entrepreneur. He lives in Glendora, California, with his wife, Gale, and has an adult daughter. Paul works a full-time job as a civil engineer. He enjoys sailing and woodworking as hobbies. Please watch for further material from Paul as he starts exploring and sharing his observations of life and world from his unique perspective. He can be reached at pjbarbe@gmail.com.

www.theknauticallife.com

40-Year Journey to Success—
Persistence Wins the Day

Craig Batley

My mother and father raised my three sisters and me during the 1950s and early 1960s. It was a simpler time, a carefree environment, instilling discipline, hard work, and a job well done in the home of my childhood.

My parents were children of the Great Depression, where one learned to pay cash for everything, if you borrowed tools you returned them in better condition than when you received them, and you respected your elders.

You also took pride in being self-sufficient, independent, and thrifty. My father taught me early in childhood the principle of being rewarded for a job well done. My parents planted the seeds for my future success. I put those principles to work by mowing yards in the summer, having a paper route, and collecting the monthly subscription fees from my customers. My first real job was working at a service station for $1.50/hour. I had many other jobs during my college years.

While in college, I began to see the possibility of business success for myself. After graduating with a BA in Business Administration, two years later I obtained an MBA emphasizing entrepreneurship, and I was ready to interview for a job with an eye toward future success. After five interviews and personality profile testing, I knew the corporate world was not for me.

I didn't want my future salary to be dictated or limited by corporate bureaucracy. I desired pay commensurate to my income producing performance. In the early 1970s, Bob Bebee was the most productive and highest paid salesman for SCM Corporation. He quit his job to become an entrepreneur, earning three times what he had been earning as the top salesman in a 1,000+ sales force. I modeled Bob Bebee.

Another early mentor, Frank Satter, told me, "You get what you ask for in life." I didn't fully understand what he meant until years later, but I decided to follow my heart (listening to that "still small voice") and struck out on my own. I didn't know what I was going to do, but I knew whatever it was I would be living in Southern California. Sometimes we don't know our ultimate destination, but our journey begins with that first step of faith. I had that yearning desire (not quite burning yet, but beginning to smolder) to break free from the yoke of predictability and family expectations. I decided to pursue possibility thinking instead of probability thinking. I made the decision to pack up and move from the Pacific Northwest in 1972 to Southern California—the land of opportunity—and ended up in Newport Beach.

There I met my next mentor and employer, a successful independent millionaire entrepreneur named Rudy Mariman. Rudy taught me the art of making cold calls—an invaluable business sales skill. After two years of apprenticeship with Rudy, I ventured out on my own as a novice real estate flipper.

I started buying and selling houses and small income properties. After hundreds of phone calls and a little elbow grease, my first "fixer" property turned a $42,000 profit.

I was on my way to becoming a millionaire through real estate investing, the proud owner of a dozen properties. However, I stopped listening to that "still small voice" and took a 13-year detour going into debt and opened real estate brokerage offices beginning in 1978. After years of owning real estate offices, closing thousands of real estate transactions, I unloaded my thriving, but marginally profitable, multimillion dollar company in 1991. After paying off debt, there wasn't much left. I was no longer a millionaire and had to start over.

Prior to making decisions, it helps if you listen to that "still small voice," or that "whisper"—if you listen, good results will always occur. I made the decision to stay in the real estate business, entering the arena of property management, a cash flow business.

With a partner, we bought a small company in 1997 on the Balboa Peninsula in Newport Beach, a company that had been in business continuously in the same location since 1967. Almost 18 years later, the business has grown by 800 percent, and we own the property on which the business began 48 years ago.

What are the lessons to be learned from my 40 years in the business? The five basic lessons I have learned to become a successful entrepreneur are:

Lesson one. Never ever go into personal debt. In other words, it is not wise to borrow your way to success. Does that mean one cannot sell equity shares in your company? No. Does that mean one should not seek venture capital? No. There are exceptions, but ideally, I recommend not being personally liable for business debt. Instead, grow organically. Grow your company to success.

Lesson two. Especially, in the beginning, learn to ask for the order. Sell your product 24/7. If you cannot sell your product, then who can? Become your company's best advocate for your product or service.

Lesson three. Be persistent. Persistence wins the prize every time. Never give up. Believe you have the best product or service. Make dozens of calls a day. Sell, then sell some more.

Lesson four. Hire good people. Hire employees who are team players. Hire people who believe in you. Hire people who complement your skills. Hire people who are enthusiastic and want the company to be successful.

Lesson five. We live in a technological world. We must innovate and stay ahead of the competition.

How did I become a 43-year "overnight" success? I became a success by dogged determination and overcoming all the obstacles and setbacks that seemingly block the road to all those who seek success. Success is something you grow into after learning from your mistakes. Along the way I made hundreds of mistakes. Remember, success can be just around the corner, it can be the next phone call or next appointment. Do not give up. Do not procrastinate. Make that phone call today. Persistent action will bring success to you, too.

Established in 1967, Craig Batley owns Burr White Realty, a boutique full service real estate office specializing in vacation rentals, property management, and sales in Newport Beach and Orange County California.

www. BurrWhite.com

Infinite Possibilities

Michelle Calloway

It was dark and the waves crashed over me. Wave after wave kept coming, devouring me. I gasped for air as I tried to keep my head above the water. I heard a voice yell in the distance, "Grab hold!" I managed to see that a boat had pulled up alongside me. A man threw a ring buoy my way, and it landed twelve inches in front of me. I tried to lift my arm out of the water to grab hold of the buoy, but I couldn't muster the strength. My arms felt like they were filled with lead. I had been treading water, fighting so hard to stay alive. I had no strength left to grab hold of the lifeline that was right in front of me. I knew I was going to drown, and I couldn't do anything to stop it.

As I awoke from this dream, I heard God's voice (in my head) say, "Do not trust in your own strength, but trust in My strength alone." *Wow!* I thought I was trusting God. I thought I was relying on His strength. This dream made it clear that I was still relying on myself to get through this trial. I knew then that my intentions to stay close to God were not enough. I couldn't rely on my own strength to hold on to Him when I got weak and weary. I needed to graft myself into His live-giving vine. John 15:5 states: "*I am the vine; you are the branches. If you remain in me and I in you, you will bear much fruit; apart from me you can do nothing.*" By grafting myself into His vine, my strength would be renewed through Him, and whenever He moved, I would be forced to move with Him. This was the beginning of my purpose-driven life.

Prior to this dream, my faith was tested beyond its breaking point. My husband, Chuck, the love of my life, my best friend, my everything, became ill after we had been married for ten years. We had two beautiful daughters, a beautiful home, jobs we enjoyed, and life was wonderful. When he became so ill that he could no longer work, we would pray together, asking God to heal him and take away his suffering. Time after time, we prayed fervently, asking God for intervention. I held tight to the Scripture in I Corinthians 10:13 that states: "God is faithful; he will not let you be tested beyond what you can bear. But when you are tested, he will also provide a way out so that you can endure it."

When God didn't heal Chuck and he continued to suffer, I lost all patience and doubted my faith. I stopped talking to God for six months. I had nothing to say to Him. I was very angry that He wasn't healing my husband, who was obviously being tried beyond what he was capable of handling. The suffering was intense!

Without God I had no hope of anything getting better. I experienced such darkness and despair when I shut God out. I felt so hopeless. After six months of not communicating with God, I asked Him to forgive me for my wretched attitude. I needed hope! I needed to believe that things were going to be okay. Even if Chuck wasn't going to be healed, I needed to know that we were in God's loving hands. I had to accept that we don't always get to know why certain things happen. His ways are not our ways. He is God, and we are NOT! We are never alone, and God promises to see us through all things.

Chuck ended up passing away, and life was very hard for a while. That is when I had the dream about drowning that I eluded to earlier. God has been faithful, and I can tell that He is always with me. God brought me a new best friend, who later became my husband. His name is Jerry, and he is a RockStar in my eyes.

In 2012, when I owned my own graphic design agency, I was introduced to an amazing new technology called augmented reality (AR). My brain was so lit up that I couldn't sleep for two straight weeks thinking about the infinite possibilities of this technology. It became very clear that God was calling me to do something with this AR technology.

So I stepped up to the plate and began learning everything I could about AR and how to develop with it. Augmented reality (AR) technology overlays virtual content on top of real-world objects. The virtual content is viewed through an AR mobile app.

A young friend of mine came to me because she knew that I could make objects "come alive" with video, and she wanted to send her boyfriend, who was deployed overseas, a greeting card that would allow him to hear her and see her anytime he wanted. I loved the idea, so we went to work. When he received the printed card with her face on it he was very touched. When he watched it "come alive" with her talking to him on the card, it rocked him to his core! He felt the distance shrink between them and felt as if she was right there with him. He carried the card with him from that day on because it made him feel closer to her.

When I saw the powerful, heartfelt connection this technology provided, I knew it needed to get it into the hands everyone, no matter their budget. I have since created REVEALiO, Inc. to bring AR experiences to individuals and businesses alike. It has the amazing power to captivate, connect, engage, and direct audiences, taking them through the entire buyer's journey in a matter of sixty seconds.

Mine is a journey of faith into the world of technology as a female founder. God renews my strength daily and gives me the courage to press on. I simply continue to show up so He can work through me. God's plan for this business is bigger than me, and I look forward to seeing it all unfold.

Visit http://revealio.com to learn how you can use augmented reality to captivate and influence others in your life.

Michelle Calloway is a speaker, international best-selling author, and the founder and CEO of REVEALiO, Inc., an augmented reality marketing company. She is driven to success in response to a calling she believes has been placed on her life. Her goal is to make augmented reality experiences available to everyone, no matter the budget.

Michelle's background includes graphic design, visual and digital communication, small business, and technology. She combines her background of visual communication with the emerging world of augmented reality, which overlays virtual content on top of real world objects when viewed through a mobile smart device.

www.revealio.com

FURTHER AWAKENING
TO MY DESTINY

Stephen Carpenter

Remember the introductory scene in *Enter the Dragon* where Bruce Lee is teaching his student Lau and says, "Kick me," to the student, who nervously complies? Master Bruce coaches his student, who then enters the flow and executes the kicks properly. Bruce asks his student, "How did it feel?" The student replies, "Hmm, let me think," while reaching for his chin. Bruce whacks him one good and asserts, "Don't think! Feel! It is like a finger pointing a way to the moon." Lau proceeds to stare at the pointing finger of Master Bruce, who compassionately teaches, "Don't concentrate on the finger or you will miss all of the heavenly glory!"

I spent the first forty-seven years of my life accumulating information and staring at the finger. On November 8, 2013, I was awakened in an instant by the most powerful storm ever to make landfall in recorded human history. Typhoon Yolanda descended upon the Philippines with a fury that day, and my pregnant wife and baby girl were residing there in Tacloban City, right in the eye of the storm. Where was I? I was across the Pacific Ocean at a RockStar Mastermind event and working full time as an EHS professional to support my family.

The people who truly matter the most to me in life were in the most dangerous situation imaginable. We had put together the perfect plan, but the universe thought differently. Finally, after seventy-two long hours, I learned my family had survived the storm! I thank GOD Almighty for protecting and guiding my loved ones safely through the storm. Within days I flew to Cebu City and was reunited with my beautiful family. When I hugged my family at the Mactan Airport, our tears flowed in a river of gratitude and love for survival in the midst of such profound devastation.

We lost many friends and some extended family members in Typhoon Yolanda. The place where the children and families used to play became like a tree where the lovely songbirds had flown away home to safety. As brave countrymen led relief missions into the disaster zone, they saw the devastation, the suffering, the survival, and the resilience of the people. The stories that came out of the disaster zone are a testament to the powerful and heroic nature of human beings. These stories and encounters changed me on a deep level.

Many brave human beings gave their lives so that others could survive. It is phenomenal that human beings are willing to risk it all to save people they often do not even know! This is a testament to our true nature. Human beings are powerful blessed sacred spiritual beings connected intimately to source energy. I AM convinced more than ever of our divine nature. I know that human beings are wondrously made.

When Typhoon Yolanda slammed into the Philippines, I was awakened from a wave spell of conditioned mind complacency and victim consciousness. The storm literally refreshed my memory that my mission here on earth is to serve humanity in positive and beneficial ways. This is about embracing our true potential as blessed sacred infinite beings here to make our world a better place for the now and future generations.

I see now that my work as an EHS professional in the trenches of corporate America through the decades has always been aligned with my life mission. Where I previously felt corporate conflict, I can now appreciate a deeper sense of my role and its importance in the workplace. After all, I work to ensure that all employees go home safe and healthy to their families after their work shifts. When workers get hurt on the job, their families and loved ones suffer the true burden of the costs. Considering how all unplanned incidents in the workplace are preventable, this is where the tire truly hits the road. It is *all* about the family. Typhoon Yolanda showed me this beyond any theory.

In 2015 I published a concise safety leadership book entitled *Your Amazing Itty Bitty Safety Book: 15 Essential Steps for the Safe & Healthy Workplace Environment*. The book encapsulates my vision for proactive risk mitigation and articulates an approach to building and sustaining a strong safety culture in your organization. I apply the book today in the role of EHS director for a large construction company. I AM quite thankful and humbled for the opportunity there to support the team and the safety mission.

To be 100 percent honest with you, I have a dream to reforest the planet earth. This focuses on a tangible solution to an environmental health and community health catastrophe facing our world today. The multipronged reforestation mission known as the Kawayan Bamboo Reforestation Initiative focuses on healthy families and healthy ecosystems, starting in the Philippines, precisely where Typhoon Yolanda made landfall. The reforestation endeavor centers on engaging the local communities in partnership planting one billion or more propagules, seedlings, and saplings of endemic bamboo, mangrove, and hardwood species. From there we go worldwide with the action plan.

The reforestation mission seeks to provide a greater degree of protection to communities from future natural disasters while creating quality livelihood opportunities. This is especially important for the youth of today and future generations. The reforestation work aims to honor both the survivors and those people who lost their lives in Typhoon Yolanda. It represents a healing opportunity and a vital mission to support the countless families and children who are still suffering today in the eye of the storm.

I AM eternally grateful to be united with my wife, daughter, and son. I honor the epiphany of love. With a tear in my eye, I will always remember our first embrace together after Typhoon Yolanda and gazing up into the night sky to see the moon waxing in all of the heavenly glory. The teacher says to expect miracles, and miracles will happen. Thank GOD for teachers. Thank GOD for miracles. I AM Grateful. I thank you. I love you.

Stephen Carpenter, MPH, CSP, works today as an occupational and environmental health and safety (EHS) professional in corporate America. He has recently developed several stylish lines of stickers that consist of super positive vibration words with the intention of inspiring kindness, increasing compassion, and awakening consciousness among all sentient beings in our world. He is starting with himself and his best friend the 'ukulele. Stephen endeavors to fund both the Kawayan Bamboo Initiative and the world-wide reforestation mission through his BLESSED SACRED™ sticker lines.

www.BlessedSacred.com

WING AND A PRAYER

Dr. Ellen Contente

If someone had told me that my fifties would be the best years of my life, I'd have laughed in their face! Surely you jest! But crow's feet and wrinkles aside, if the next decade is anything like the last—bring it on! I've accomplished more in the past ten years than in all the years leading up to them. And I did it all on a "Wing and a Prayer."

Since turning fifty, I've gone back to school twice; received my Masters in Spiritual Psychology, then my doctorate. I became licensed as a Religious Science Practitioner and Minister with the Global Truth Center. I founded Heart-Centered Programs, my corporate training and consulting business. I've also traveled to Japan, South Africa, and Denmark, all while flying back and forth to Oklahoma to help care for my ailing mother.

As a self-starter, I've taken every seminar you can imagine on business and personal development—including walking across hot coals, sitting in a sweat lodge, and climbing the "Tower of Doom." I've created a radio show, written articles, and developed programs, including "Life Is a Balancing Act," my signature workshop. All on pretty much a "Wing and a Prayer"!

You're probably thinking, *Well, she must be single or crazy, or both!* Wrong! And (partially) wrong! Getting married and raising twins after becoming a mom at forty can make anyone crazy (so can marriage, but that's another book)! It may be common now, but back then I was the oldest mom on the block! And getting there wasn't easy.

I had to give myself daily hormone injections and *voluntarily* subject myself to mood swings, bloating, and monthly egg harvesting. Ahh . . . the downside of IVF (in-vitro fertilization). I looked like a voodoo doll with all the needle holes! Little did I know then that it would be good practice for the daily injections I would be taking for Hep-C treatments in the coming years.

I was actually diagnosed seven years prior with Hepatitis non-A/non-B, as it was called in the early nineties. Back then there was no known cure, and I was told I'd need a liver transplant to survive. Not exactly the diagnosis one wants to hear! Especially since I had no idea how I contracted it. Didn't drink (too much), didn't do drugs (does caffeine count?), and was basically a "goody two-shoes." So much for having no vices (and no fun)!

Unless you consider spending two full years sticking yourself with a needle fun! Well—my husband did most of the sticking—which was a blast for him! But it was all worth it when the stork delivered us Jesse and Jaime, healthy boy-girl twins. I started Hep-C treatment when I was done breastfeeding, and I've been virus-free ever since.

Another "Wing and a Prayer" outcome!

In the early years of motherhood, I worked as a sales manager in the technology industry selling software solutions. Translation: long, hard hours and lots of traveling. At that time, I was commuting into New York City when I wasn't on the road. That in and of itself was exhausting! Throw in taking care of two toddlers that would frequently use toothpaste and poop as "body-paint" (*at four in the morning*), a hefty mortgage, and you have a recipe for disaster! And it hit in the form of a layoff! Had I not been completely burnt out, I'd have been devastated. Instead I saw it as a blessing in disguise!

My husband and I decided to move and start over: no more grueling schedules and hopefully no more harsh winters and shoveling snow! José Antonio, my actor husband, suggested we head West to the "City of Angels," so we sold the house and our belongings and hit the road with our four-year-old twins. It was on a "Wing and a Prayer" that we arrived in Los Angeles nine months later. We were ready to birth our new life; that, and sleep in a real bed!

I became a serial entrepreneur. It would take multiple business "failures" before the success of my Heart-Centered Programs. But I was determined not to follow in my dad's footsteps. He worked his entire life only to drop dead of a heart attack within two years of retiring. I knew there must be more to life than sacrificing everything for just a few precious years of enjoyment.

I wanted Work/Life balance for myself and others, and I wasn't taking "No" for an answer! That's how Heart-Centered Programs was born.

Today I empower people to live with more Passion, Purpose and Play™. To enjoy life now and practice Inner-Balance by living in gratitude, grace, and appreciation. I work with organizations to facilitate positive work environments where people are valued and accountable for their own well-being and success.

It's about living from the inside-out, not allowing outside circumstances to dictate your results. I've learned to focus on what I want, take action, and trust that whatever I need will be there for me. Either in "form" or in the form of a lesson.

Some lessons are hard. Like bankruptcy. Like raising sensitive children going through dark times, suicide attempts, and brave new beginnings. I learned the lesson of letting go and unconditional love. And that life is precious.

Whenever I speak, whether a keynote or to a congregation, I share these messages. We can choose to live from a "heart-centered" place—no matter what's going on in our lives. Life is meant to be enjoyed, and it's never too late to try new things!

I ran my first 5K at fifty-three. I now run regularly and have only one requirement: it must be fun! I've run for chocolate, FroYo, and donuts. I ran through movie studios and back lots, past the Queen Mary and through Dodger Stadium. I was doused with colored chalk and ran through colored bubbles! I even accidentally ran in the Cape Town marathon!

I run to finish. That's my reward! To inspire and motivate myself, I'll find someone older than me who's running and keep pace with them. If they can do it, so can I!

I used to get stuck in "how am I going to ___" (fill in the blank), and that would stop me dead in my tracks. Fear. Doubt. Insecurity. Not anymore. Today I wear a wristband that says, "Say yes, and figure it out later." I've said "yes" to a lot of things—both good and not so good, but always an adventure! "Yes"—life is lived on a "Wing and a Prayer"!

Dr. Ellen Contente is the founder of Heart-Centered Programs, a training and consulting business empowering people to live and work with more Passion, Purpose and Play™. An international speaker and seminar leader, she is frequently requested for her warm engaging style and ability to connect with people at all levels of an organization. People resonate with her genuine nature and personal stories. She is the author of several upcoming books, creator of "Life is a Balancing Act" and one-woman show, "When Bad Blonde Happens to Good Brunette." She currently resides in Los Angeles with her husband and eighteen-year old twins.

www.HeartCenteredPrograms.com

God or Good Fortune?

Ken Courtright

I was deep into a Brian Tracy book when I read about the principle of 10X growth. In short, Brian explained that one of the fastest ways for your business to grow tenfold was to reengineer your company to be led by a person that was the head of a corporation ten times bigger than your current company.

At the time my wife Kerri and I owned a few businesses. We agreed that for each business to grow to the size we desired, we would need to find people currently leading companies significantly larger than ours.

With that in mind, we made the decision that we weren't going to stop interviewing people until we found the perfect person to run each entity. We gave ourselves one caveat. The people we brought in must be currently leading a company ten times our size.

In under thirty days we found the perfect person to run our first company. We shared our vision with this person, and within one week of meeting him, he and his wife agreed to leave the state they lived in and move to Illinois to help us grow our small business.

This is where our story gets interesting.

You see, this gentleman left his comfortable job of ten years to come to our fledgling company. During his second week at the helm, we ran into a bit of a financial hardship.

On the Monday of his second week on the job, I took a call from someone stating that the large check that was to be deposited with us this morning would be delayed . . . indefinitely. This happened to be the check that was scheduled and budgeted to cover our next six payrolls.

This caused a bit of a challenge.

How was I going to tell this man—who just left his job of ten years, leading a stable and still growing company—that, well, he wasn't going to get his first paycheck?

Completely shell-shocked and in a state of denial, I sat at my desk, took a deep breath, and said the following:

"Lord, I'm guessing you didn't send me to southern Indiana to extract a great man out of a perfectly good job to come run our company only to miss his first payroll."

I went on to say, verbatim, "God, I don't know how you are going to pull this off, but I'm going to give you until Thursday at 3:00 p.m. to figure it out. At 3:00 p.m. on Thursday, I'll let everyone know that nobody is getting paid on Friday."

At that, I left my office and went to work on whatever project was scheduled for that day.

The next day, Tuesday, was a bit of a blur due to a large fabrication issue we ran into at one of our facilities. Wednesday was similar, as I got a call that had something to do with us accidentally installing a piece of equipment on the wrong side of a building's driveway. Tuesday and Wednesday flew by.

I remember waking up on Thursday and going about my morning as scheduled until I tried to use my debit card for gas. It was declined. Reality hit me like steam engine.

I stood staring at the gas pump for quite some time. I dug out the change that was in the ashtray, put a couple bucks of gas in the tank, and went to the office.

Like Tuesday and Wednesday, due to having multiple businesses, the urgent instantly distracted me from the important. I was again sucked into the mayhem of a typical day back then.

At 2:59 p.m. my cell phone rang.

"Is this Ken?"

"Who is this?" I asked.

"Ken, it's your banker, Tom, across the street. Last time you were in, you wrote your new cell number down on your business card. Is this a bad time?"

Trying to decide if I should laugh or cry, I softly said, "I've got a minute— what's up?"

"Do you remember the last time you were here?"

With a sarcastic laugh, I said, "Yes, the time when I asked for a large line of credit and you laughed me out of your office because of how young we were and the types of companies we ran. Do you mean that visit?"

He replied, "Exactly, yes. The funny thing is that our group met this morning and you and Kerri came up. We noticed in your accounts that you have had loans for numerous vehicles and other items and have always paid us on time, if not even early. We came out of our meeting wondering if you still needed that line of credit."

It was at this point, stunned, that I remembered my conversation with my Friend upstairs.

Smiling, and not quite able to control myself, I said, "Tom, if you are serious, how long would it take to actually receive the line of credit?"

It was his turn to laugh a bit. "How long would it take you to get here?"

Knowing he knew I could see his building from my front window, I said, "Maybe five minutes."

His reply, "If you can be here in five minutes and sign a few docs, I could probably have the money in your account by 3:30."

I almost dropped the phone.

Thinking on my feet a bit, I did two things in the next few minutes.

First, knowing I was going to someday share this story with my kids and grandkids, I took a picture of my phone, with the inbound call showing the banker's name, phone number, and the time stamp of 2:59 p.m.

Second, I jogged across the street.

True to his word, I had docs signed and funds to cover many payrolls and then some in the next half hour.

For years, nobody, not even my incredible wife, Kerri, knew how close we came to a real embarrassment.

Was it God or good fortune? You decide.

––––––––––––––––

Ken Courtright is the founder and CEO of the four-time Inc. 5000 company, Income Store. Income Store has helped hundreds of families and businesses add immediate revenue to their households through revenue-generating websites. Ken's company now manages and shares revenue on over 800 moneymaking websites.

A best-selling author *in five categories*, Ken has been featured on WLS, FOX, CBS, A&E, in *Forbes*, and most recently on the Biography Channel.

With a website portfolio viewed over 400 million times each year, Income Store has doubled revenues five years in a row, placing them on the Inc. 5000 list in 2013, 2014, 2016, and again this year.

www.IncomeStore.com

YOU ARE RESPONSIBLE FOR YOUR LIFE

Kerri Courtright

Success is a real big word. I discovered that at the age of five. While most kids liked to play with Barbies and color in coloring books, I enjoyed hanging out with the adults. I was an only child of two teenagers. The reason they married is pretty obvious. My parents were, and are, amazing. Back then they had nothing, and nothing is what I was used to. However, at the young age of five, I could see there were differences in my life versus the lives of others. My earliest recollection was waking up in my small bed. I later was informed that my bedroom was a closet in the one-bedroom apartment my parents shared.

When asked what I'd like to be when I grew up, I told people I wanted to be a lawyer. It was a lawyer who owned the biggest, most beautiful house on the lake where my grandparents had a small, two-bedroom cottage. It had a bathroom with a sink, toilet, and no shower. The lake was our bathtub.

A word I consistently heard growing up was *no*. No, you don't need that. No, we can't afford that. No, just because everyone else has that doesn't mean you need it. No, I'm sorry, you can only have one ballet class. No, we just don't have the money.

In fourth and fifth grade, kids called me "Kmart Kerri" since that was the only store my parents shopped at for all my clothes. Nicknames stay with you all your life; they can tear you down or be great motivators.

In life, you always have at least two choices. Either accept where you are and stay there, or change your course to where you want to go and become who you want to be. My desire at the age of five was to do whatever it took to have enough discretionary income to be able to have choices; though that might not have been my vocabulary at the time, it was my mentality. I wanted the ability to choose where I shopped, drink soda pop if I desired, or buy a car that didn't come with a rusted bottom.

My success story is that I became a "scrapper." It's a term of endearment to me. My husband likes to say that I "will" things to happen. So be it—I accept the words of affirmation. My motto was "whatever it takes."

In my teens, I was an independent contractor for fitness clubs. Making my own hours and setting my own wages was a thrilling new experience. This is how I paid my way through college. At the end of college, my boyfriend (soon to be husband) and I began our first company. It started with Ken selling signs and me making and shipping them.

We often worked through the night to make sure the signs were completed on time. This commitment meant many missed family functions and get-to-gethers with friends. This all paid off. Soon we had fantastic sales and our own manufacturing teams. Things were so good that we decided to widen our scope of business to include a passion. We loved to relax after work and watch movies in our living room, so we began opening video stores.

Things were great in the beginning. We had three fantastic video stores in great locations. Things were so good that even Blockbuster and Hollywood Video thought they could make some money. They set up a location one block from each of ours and their pockets were deeper than ours. To keep our video stores competing against the chain movie stores, we started taking money from the sign company to purchase more videos. The effort was good but, ultimately, we closed all video stores *and* the sign company.

Tangibly, we lost everything. Our employees, who believed in us, were out of jobs. We had no income. I was pregnant. My greatest fears of possibly losing our financial independence and having to raise my child under the financial stress that my parents raised me, was daunting. The years of "Kmart Kerri" came rushing to the forefront of my mind.

The thing is, though, what we lost were just tangible goods. We had learned what to do and what not to do. We discovered that we worked great together and could rely on each other. We knew that this was temporary and there was a much bigger plan for us.

When our businesses closed, we took time to regroup both as a couple and as business partners. Thinking through our business years, we realized that we had been giving out business tips to those who purchased signs from us. We made a pivot. The signs that were made for the business owners were just a part of helping them in their growth. There were other things that we could do to help them, expanding beyond the physical signs for their companies. Our business morphed into consulting. As time and techniques changed, we changed with them. When the Internet became user-friendly, we jumped in.

My husband and I now own TGC / Income Store, and today my wardrobe is filled with designer attire.

During all the early turmoil, we could have fought each other. We could have both gotten jobs. We could have . . .

Because I am a scrapper, I chose to fight. Our loss was just a temporary setback, something to learn from. It was simply time for a new goal.

It was a pivotal moment to realize how quickly things can change and the need to change with them.

The thing is . . . *the experiences of my youth became my fuel for success.*

It never crossed my mind to succumb and surrender. We all have choices. We can choose to fight for something or choose to fight to get away from something. Surrender is not an option. Each person has something amazing they are destined to do. Age and money are not prerequisites or limits.

Kerri Courtright is the co-founder of the Inc. 5000 company Income Store. Income Store helps people and businesses grow their income through building or buying revenue-generating websites.

Kerri runs Digital Footprint, their business growth conference that both *Forbes* and *Inc.* rank as one of the Top Five "Can't Miss" business conferences in North America.

Kerri, a former Chicago Bulls cheerleader, is now a best-selling author and elected official in Illinois.

After doubling revenues five years in a row (in 2013, 2015, 2016, and now again in 2017), their twenty-four-year-old company is ranked in *Inc.* magazine as one of the 1,000 Fastest Growing U.S. Companies.

www.IncomeStore.com

but the best for my former partner. There are over 7 billion people in the world, so there is enough for all of us.

Through all the pain, I have arrived at a very peaceful place. By getting silent and listening to my heart and my head, I've learned what it means to trust myself. There is no substitute for having your head and your heart in alignment. When I smile today, I feel my heart smiling too.

My new business, Beauty Boss Network, is a reflection of the real me, and it has attracted team members, corporate sponsors, mentors, and customers who I am in alignment with on so many levels. Everything I have today is a result of what I have been through. The tough times and hard lessons didn't happen *to* me; they happened *for* me. I realize that it is possible to build an amazingly successful business while also living in happiness.

The journey has been worth it. It's scary to travel into the darkness. Yet you have to know that darkness is a great teacher. Knowing what darkness is helps you to truly appreciate the light. And, when you give yourself permission to get silent so that you can listen to your heart, you end up illuminating the pathway for others too. This is perhaps the greatest happiness of all.

Briana Dai is a sought-after international makeup artist and hairstylist, entrepreneur, event producer, podcast host, author, and social media influencer. She works with major brands, including James Avery, Bloomingdale's, ESPN The Body Issue, Famous Footwear, and more. Briana's experience in the beauty industry ranges from working as a national trainer for cosmetic retail brands, television networks, celebrities such as Mariah Carey, LeAnn Rimes, Martina Navratilova, the Dallas Cowboys cheerleaders, and Ezekiel Elliott to everyday clients. Today she is the CEO of Beauty Boss Network, a powerful networking and resource company dedicated to serving the needs of beauty industry professionals.

www.BeautyBossNetwork.com

LIVE WITHIN YOUR MEANS

Anne and Anton Duswalt

Anne

I was born in Bronx, New York, with three other siblings—two older sisters and one younger brother. My parents were immigrants, born in Ireland, and came here to the United States to be married because they were of different religious backgrounds and that was frowned upon in Ireland.

I went to eight different schools and moved around quite a bit. We settled in Kew Gardens, New York, and I graduated from high school. After high school I worked in New York City as a secretary for a factoring company, then at TWA, and ultimately at a dental office for most of my adult life.

Anton

I was born in Brooklyn, New York, with an older sister, younger brother, and younger sister, and my family settled in Ozone Park, New York. I graduated from high school and immediately joined the Air Force for four years during the Korean War. After my four-year stint in the service, I worked for a printing company and then had a long career with a telephone company on Long Island as a switchman and a troubleshooter.

Our Story

We met at Anton's ski club's cocktail party. We were engaged one year later and married six months after that. We settled in an apartment in Ozone Park, New York. Eighteen months later we were blessed with our first child, a baby boy we named Craig. We moved to Long Island and bought a modest home in Deer Park, where we were blessed with our daughter, Pamela, twenty months later.

We were never rich, but we were always comfortable. But what is rich, really?

We had an amazing group of friends and were very involved with our kid's sports and our church. This is how we had fun. It wasn't going to fancy restaurants in New York City; it wasn't traveling the world—we were happy watching our son play football and our daughter cheer on Sundays. After the games we would go to friend's homes and just hang out.

We also ran the church variety shows every year. One year we sang a Sonny and Cher song, where Anne was Sonny and Anton was Cher. We had a blast. Our kids would watch all the rehearsals while doing their homework. They loved it.

All this revolved around having fun with our family and friends. And it did not cost a lot of money. The world is so different now, and we hope, for the sake of our kids, that they enjoy their families as much as we did.

So what is rich? Rich is never having to worry about money. Not that we had a ton of it, but we were taught by our parents at a very early age that you should never live beyond your means.

After many years of paying cash for everything, we finally applied for a charge account and were pleased to get one. We mainly used it to establish credit. But we were careful, and we paid our bills every month. If we knew we couldn't pay our bills one month, and we wanted to buy something, we would wait until we could afford it and then charge it.

We have been married for more than fifty-seven years, and we have never paid interest on anything except our house and one car. Oh, and we paid $15,800 for our house, and we still live in it.

While it might have been nice to eat at more expensive restaurants, take more vacations, and tour the world in a private jet, none of that really ever interested us. But because of that, we are proud to say that we will never outlive our money. And there is a huge comfort in that.

We are also very lucky and proud to have two very successful children, who we have been informed, both live within their means. At least that's what they tell us. Their bills are a lot higher than ours ever were, but we understand that it's a whole new world. However, I think they both learned from us, as we did from our parents, to enjoy family and friends first, and not so much the materials things.

As you are well aware by now, Craig is the main author of this book. We were so grateful when Craig asked us to write a little story for this book about a success that we've had.

Well, after wrestling what to write about, we decided that our two biggest successes are our two children.

Craig currently lives in California with his beautiful wife and amazing (and handsome) three boys. But before all this, he graduated from SUNY Oswego with a marketing degree, and then toured with Air Supply and Guns N' Roses, which freaked us out. But we met the members of both the bands, and we're happy to say, they were awesome to our son. Russell Hitchcock, the lead singer of Air Supply, still calls us to this day and gets us tickets to his concerts whenever they come to Long Island. Thank you, Russell.

We have been to many of Craig's RockStar Marketing BootCamps in Los Angeles. Every time we attend, his attendees make us feel like we're the Rock-Stars. His audiences are filled with amazing, wonderful, and caring people. We are blown away every time we go.

Our daughter, Pamela, graduated college with a business degree, and is a former model, a former New Jersey General's cheerleader, and is currently enjoying her life as a teacher's assistant at a private school in Florida. She is married to William Malinchak, a former NFL Football player for the Washington Redskins and a commodities trader. They have three beautiful daughters and one handsome son.

We have both lived a very blessed life and for that, we are grateful. Anne will continue shopping at flea markets and garage sales, and Anton loves building birdhouses for the 1.2 million birds in our backyard. And we will continue enjoying our lives and our children.

A ROCKSTAR STRATEGY THROUGH THE VOICE OF GOD?

Maryann Ehmann

I was so tired of it. Literally. My mind and body ached from sleepless nights worrying about our dwindling finances. Losing our home and living in a cardboard box under a bridge was looking more and more like our future reality. I'm not exaggerating.

Just a few years prior, we had taken the leap and moved into our country estate with lush and bountiful gardens, manicured lawns, and wildlife to greet us each morning. This property was beyond my dreams. Meeting the higher mortgage and expenses was no problem, as our business more than supported the increase.

Life was good.

And then, to our horror, 9/11 occurred. As with many others, fear invaded our hearts, while we watched the devastation. It became clear that the attack on the world's financial center was strategically designed to cripple the finances of the US, but never did we expect to personally feel the ripple in our business. One by one, my husband lost his insurance company clients as they decided to discontinue using outside investigators to cut costs.

At first we thought this shift was just another little dip in the road from which we would recover in a short period, just as we had so many other times. Business has its ups and downs, and typically, if you stay positive, plan, and adjust, the road smooths out eventually.

But one month turned into six, which turned into twelve, and after three years of income one-third of what it had been, we could no longer stave off the creditors or rob Peter to pay Paul. Peter was broke.

One thing about ongoing crisis is it can bring you to your knees in desperate prayer, and believe me we were doing that as we sought a strategy to change things.

But nothing was changing.

Our old methods of seeking God's help were no longer working. "What the heck?" I felt abandoned, alone, and victimized by an economy we couldn't control.

"What are we missing? It's not supposed to be this way! We both have doctorates, for crying out loud!" More self-pity and resentment clouded my mind.

And then a moment of clarity came: I saw that my faith was not in an upward swing but in our inevitable decline.

"As your faith is, so shall it be."

Faith has a direction, and I did not like where ours was headed.

So we studied the will of God about finances, prosperity, and business success and learned that our mind-sets were messed up! It wasn't the economy that was the problem; it was our beliefs! This revelation empowered me. Faith rose up that relief would come. I didn't know how or when, but for the first time in years, I was certain a solution would appear.

One day while listening to one of our favorite teachers share how his wife secured just the right job after writing down her requirements, something spoke to my soul. Could it be that we could actually write down our desires and . . . get them? That seemed wrong. I had been warned about treating God like a Santa Claus. Was that what this teacher was promoting?

Not at all. I realized in that instant, that God had already given us all the provisions for an abundant life, and our job was to access it. Not beg, borrow, or steal. But simply access it.

Just at that moment, a gentle whisper instructed my heart, saying, "Write down how much you and Gene want and don't skimp. I am a God of more than enough, and it is all yours."

Filled with excitement and apprehension, I ran to Gene and told him what I had heard. "You write down an amount, and I will, too, and let's see if they are the same!" And so we did.

Thinking about all the things that had fallen into disrepair, the mounting debt, not being able to visit our daughter and family in England, "go big or go home" raced through my mind like I was writing our ticket to Adventure Land. I didn't second guess it, refusing to even think what my husband might write.

OMG! It was exactly the same as mine.

A few days later my husband received a contract for work that would cover fifty percent of the dollar amount to which we were committed. Though it increased our current revenues, and it was an "out of the blue" offer, it wasn't enough to match the amount we had written. He declined.

"Was this craziness? Turning down an offer that was almost twice as much as our current income?"

No, it was wisdom. To follow the voice of God and His leading seems nuts in our day and age. But is it?

We are smart people. But our smarts did not keep us from getting into a deep financial hole or help find a way to get us out.

No. We needed something bigger than ourselves.

We needed an out of the box, RockStar strategy.

Who knew it would be through the voice of God?

Confidence and peace replaced my anxiety-riddled nights, even before the money was in the bank! My husband put a stake in the ground when he said no. And guess what? They came back with another 25 percent increase. The remaining 25 percent came easy with my help.

After years of inadequate revenues, more than 100 percent of our number came into our bank accounts each and every month. Following that, we received even more.

We paid off debt, repaired and improved the house, took a wonderful family trip to Europe (two, in fact), purchased sorely needed new cars, and abounded in excess of our expenses.

Unbeknownst to us, God was giving us the keys to manifesting our dreams and desires: Honor them, listen to Him, set your intention, and take action. As our renewed mind-set has continued to upgrade, so has our life. Change your beliefs, change your results!

———————————

Maryann Ehmann is a professional speaker, radio show host, success coach, and creator of Create Your Magnificent Life Now. Maryann inspires and coaches entrepreneurs, professionals, and ministry leaders to live a life beyond their dreams by strengthening the beliefs they need to achieve the results they desire.

www.MaryannEhmann.com

DETERMINATION

Geri England

Have you ever wanted something so much that you knew you would never give up until you got it? That describes how I felt about going to college. I wanted to go to college more than anything I have ever wanted in my entire life. This desire intensified all through my teen years.

The things that fueled my quest? An abusive home life, a yearning for a better life, and an eagerness to learn.

When I was two years old, my father suffered acute appendicitis and almost died. He developed multiple blood clots in his legs. The doctors tied off the arteries to his legs and put him on blood thinners. After that, he developed a serious health problem (thrombophlebitis) that affected him for the rest of his life.

Not only did he suffer physical pain, but he also bore deep emotional anguish from the loss of his dreams. He drowned his bitterness and resentment in alcohol. Maybe because I resisted, I experienced the brunt of his ravings. He was critical and abusive, often yelling and cursing at me.

My saving grace was school—a respite from the harshness at home. I loved school from the very first day. I excelled and thrived there. My mother supported me with my homework and school activities, and two teachers took a special interest in me and encouraged me. In high school, I was fortunate to attend honors classes and be named to the honor society. I made the drill team and became president of my Junior Achievement company.

I'm not sure how old I was when I made this decision, but I decided that no matter what it took, I was going to college. I wanted out of that negative, repressive home environment. I wanted something better for myself—to be on my own, to learn about the world, and to get an education. College was my key to freedom and a more positive future.

As my father aged, his health deteriorated, limiting his ability to work. My mother went to work, and we lived on her small salary and my father's government pension. While we had a roof over our heads and enough to eat, we had little money for much else.

My father's plan for me was similar to my mother's path—secretarial school. They had no money for me to attend college. I had other plans.

The last semester of my senior year, I began looking for jobs. The bus I rode to school traveled through downtown Dallas, the location of lots of businesses. Every week, after school I'd hop off the bus, visit different offices, and inquire about job openings. A manager at First National Bank told me they hired trainee operators for their transit department. Once I learned that, I bugged him every week.

"Mr. Smith, do you have any trainee openings yet?"

"Sorry, we don't have any openings right now. Check back in a few weeks."

My persistence paid off, because the week before I graduated from high school, Mr. Smith offered me a job. On June 3rd at age eighteen, I started my first job at the whopping salary of $220 per month. My plan was to save all my money for college. Then I got a surprise: My father began charging me rent (seventy-five dollars a month) because I was now an adult and must pay my way. I stashed every other dollar I could into my savings.

Maybe I can save enough money to enroll in college in a year or so, I thought.

One day in August a girlfriend from church called me and said, "Are you still interested in going to college?"

"Are you kidding? Yes!"

Nancy said, "If you take a day off work, I'll drive you to my university and help you explore financial options for this fall."

I was thrilled beyond belief. "Yes!"

Without telling my parents, I embarked on this adventure with Nancy.

In the financial aid office, we learned about a math/science scholarship fund. I filled out an application, declared myself a math major, and received a small scholarship. I couldn't believe it!

Next stop: the job center. As I explained my situation, Dr. Franklin, Psychology Department chairman, overheard my story.

"I've got two openings for secretaries earmarked for financially needy students. If you want a job, you can have it."

I was so excited! This meant I had just enough money (barely) to go to college for a year!

Back home I braced myself for my father's reaction as I laid out my plan.

"Daddy, I want to go to college."

"Damn it. I told you. You can't go to college. We don't have the money."

"Daddy, my friend Nancy helped me today. I landed a job and a scholarship, and I have $420 in savings. It's enough money to pay for books, dorm, and tuition."

"Well, I'll be damned. I guess you can go."

I was beside myself with excitement!

Nancy threw me a "bon voyage" party with friends and family. I received clothes, cash, and other items. I almost cried when I opened Nancy's gift: a pair of shoes and a note. I felt embarrassed about needing shoes. But the note stunned me. *Nancy's family offered to pay for my college!* They had lost another daughter to a cerebral hemorrhage at the age of fifteen. They had a college fund for her. What an unbelievably kind gesture!

"Nancy, I appreciate your generous offer, but I can't accept it. It's too much. You showed me how and now I can do it myself."

I did put myself through college (the first in my family) by working part-time twenty-five hours a week and through summer jobs. Later I completed a master's degree and created a successful career. My gruff father bragged about me and then "expected" my sister to go to college. My parents didn't know anything beyond their own world view. Thus, I became the trailblazer, opening their eyes, and mine, to new possibilities with the help of a friend.

I learned to create a clear intention for what I want, pursue it with dogged determination, and accept help from angels along the way.

Geri England, MS, Med, is the founder of Positive Change Workz and creator of Discover Your Story to Success© System. She is a business and story coach, trainer, speaker, author, and organization development consultant. She also serves on the faculty of the University of Texas-Dallas. Geri helps clients discover and leverage the power of their stories so they can create positive change, influence others, achieve personal breakthroughs, and reinvent themselves. As a result, they implement smart strategies to grow their businesses/careers while making a difference. Geri leads signature workshops on business storytelling, coaching skills, and appreciative inquiry and facilitates corporate leadership/team development processes.

www.PositiveChangeWorkz.com

Fighting the Good Fight of Faith

Vivian R. England

There was a time when things in my life began to become topsy-turvy. I had been going through spiritual warfare on the job for years. I suffered a miscarriage, which almost took my mind. Then, my marriage began to fall apart, after my mother-in-law passed away, having been married to her son for only four years. It was as if the man I married died with his mother, because he completely shut down. There was no more communication between us, or if there was any, it was very limited. Yet when he got around his friends, especially in the church, he seemed to come alive.

As time progressed, matters seemed to get worse. My husband became more distant, until I felt as though I only had a roommate. I was being attacked from the left and the right. Every day I would go into my private chambers and war against the enemy through prayer. Spirits of depression, anxiety, and low self-esteem tried to attach themselves to me and hurl me into a state of bondage. One day the Lord awakened me and told me that it wasn't anything wrong with me; it was something wrong with my husband. He could not go where the Lord was carrying me. Those words of the Lord gave me comfort and peace of mind. The enemy became defeated!

My mind reflected back on how many times the enemy tried to take my life. At the age of three months, I was plagued with chicken pox from one of my older siblings. My mother tells me I had such a terrible bout, I almost died—defeated. At the age of five months, another older sibling had a pillow and was just getting ready to smother me when my mother entered the room just in the nick of time—defeated. On another occasion, while I was sitting in my walker, my mother happened to enter the room and that same sibling had placed a diaper over my head, still trying to smother me—defeated.

Later, in the eighth grade, I found myself in an altercation at school that resulted in my getting stitches in the back of my head. One of my classmates went around telling people she was going to come to school the next day to kick my butt. Why? To this day, it is beyond my comprehension. However, during the altercation, the children in the class said, "Uh-oh, she's got a knife!" My mind went through this dialogue: "What are they talking about? I don't have a knife. Oh, *she's* got a knife! Well, you better get the best of her." It seemed like the two of us had been fighting for quite some time. Finally, my teacher pulled me from off the top of her. The girl jumped up and headed straight for the door. The teacher summoned her back, but she refused and proceeded out the door. He turned to me and said, "You're cut. I'm taking you down to the nurse's office."

As we were walking down the hallway, I felt something trickling down the back of my head. When I drew my hand back, there was blood on my fingers. I stated, "She cut me in the back of my head." Arriving at the nurse's office, she accessed the situation and indicated that I needed stitches. My mother came to the school and drove me to George Washington Hospital (GW). At GW, the nurse prepped the area and the doctor sutured the area. When he was finished, the doctor said, "You are lucky, young lady! If it was an inch deeper, you would have died." I don't believe in luck, I believe in God! The enemy was defeated once again. Hallelujah!

Know that the enemy will use anyone—whether foe or family—to try and take us out. However, the Bible says:

Finally, my brethren, be strong in the Lord, and in the power of His might. Put on the whole armour of God, that ye may be able to stand against the wiles of the devil. For we wrestle not against flesh and blood, but against principalities, against powers, against the rulers of the darkness of this world, against spiritual wickedness in high places. (Ephesians 6:10–12, KJV)

It is never the individual that we are warring against; we are in a constant spiritual warfare. However, we can always come out victoriously if we keep the faith and hold to God's unchanging hand. Hebrews 11:1 says, "Now faith is the substance of things hoped for, the evidence of things not seen."

"Now faith is" is expressing a fact about the present, whereas "of things hoped for" is directed toward the future. So according to this Scripture, we can safely say that the things we hope to possess in the future are brought nigh by our present faith. Our present faith will bring a manifestation of the invisible things not yet seen.

No matter what happens in your life, hold on to your faith in God! If you don't have a relationship with Him, get to know Him. Romans 8:28 says, "And we know that all things work together for good to them that love God, to them who are the called according to His purpose."

Everyone on the face of this earth was born with a purpose. It doesn't matter whether your mother's pregnancy was planned or not; God has a plan for your life. No one can fulfill that plan except you. Get in the Word of God and develop a relationship with Him through prayer and His Word. Ask Him, "God, what is the plan for my life?"

God revealed to me His plan for my life. That's why I fight the good fight of faith, against all odds. Before leaving this earth, I aim to fulfill my purpose. I encourage you to do the same. Fight the good fight of Faith!

———————

Vivian R. England—The Voice of Inspiration—is a native Washingtonian, an international speaker, author, sign language interpreter, community advocate, spiritual counselor, and ordained minister. She has a passion for the Deaf, seniors, young children, single mothers, and those less fortunate. Having survived many setbacks in life, her mission is to reach out to help other hurting women. Her desire is to let them know they can rise above the pain, hurt, and agony to embrace a newfound love, joy, and peace that lies within. Her contact information is: P.O. Box 7137, Largo, MD 20792.

living4purpose@yahoo.com

LIFE IS A JOURNEY

Paul Finck

Life is a journey . . . at least my life has been. From start to well, not quite finished yet, my life has been an incredible journey—almost an epic novel. The latest incredible chapter started in 2001. My name is Paul Finck, The Maverick Millionaire®, and a little over fifteen years ago, my last set of twins were born. This is where my story begins. This key event gave me the motivation and dedication to create a powerful new journey for myself and my family.

Yes, I did say my last set of twins! I have three sets of twins—six children in total. Amanda and Alexandra are my oldest girls. They are adopted (my nieces biologically). My wife and I have cherished and cared for them every second from the moment they were born. Then came Stephen and Katerina. They were born via in vitro fertilization (IVF). And four months later, surprise! My wife was pregnant again (the old-fashioned way) with David and Daniel, my identical boys. Three boys, three girls—The Brady Bunch comes to life.

So now what?

I had been in straight commissions sales, marketing, and entrepreneurship since 1986. What I realized quickly as I went from a family of four to a family of eight within fourteen months is that I had to do things differently, and by quite a sum. I looked up the income range for participating in financial aid in my part of the country (the amount of money you could be earning or less to still qualify for food stamps). For a family of eight, I could be earning as much as $73,000 and still qualify. I did not realize how close to poverty level I was at the time. I just knew I had to create more, and quickly! So I decided to get educated.

I had heard on the radio of this program by . . . wait . . . hold your breath, all you experienced real estate investors . . . Carleton Sheets, the famous real estate investor/ no money down guru from the seventies. He had a CD set for sale, and as I was driving one day from account to account, I heard the advertisement and wrote down the number. Well, this program was an incredible, outrageous $800. To me at the time, wow, holy smokes, that was a lot of money. I had six kids and a wife to answer to. I couldn't buy this—at least not without asking first! So, I dug deep for my best sales material and went to work on convincing my wife this was our answer!

Now, I don't know about the rest of the guys out there, but I know myself. If my wife was not 100 percent on board with the program—with this new step in our incredible journey—there was no way it was going to work. Effective communication would be a must. Working as a team was necessary, along with the complete understanding of what all this was going to mean to our future and what we were going to have to give up to make it work.

I can hear some of you already "What do you mean, I have to 'give up' something? I was told I could have all I want. Life is abundant. This is an 'and' world, not an 'either/or' world."

As true as all these beliefs are, often momentary sacrifice is necessary. I have found this especially true in transition periods in your journey. The biggest sacrifices must be made to create the biggest changes . . . and the biggest rewards.

As my wife and I talked, we came to an agreement. Yes, my wife and I came to an agreement before we started down this new path together. She agreed to take on the majority of the care taking of the children. Before this time, I was fifty/fifty partners with her on everything. She did the laundry. I did all the food shopping. She cooked. I cleaned the dishes. We both fed, fed, fed the babies. We both changed, changed, changed all the diapers. Now things had to change for us to simply survive. I told her, "Give me twelve months." In twelve months, I promised her that I would work the system, take action, and create a new vision for our life! I would continue my current job and on nights, weekends, and anytime in between, I would work on creating abundance via real estate investing. OK, great pitch . . . now I had to go out and do it, which really scared me to the core. The "what if" mambo was going off in my head.

We were planning a trip to go to Florida with the whole family to visit my wife's brother and Mickey Mouse. From our house in Connecticut, this was a twenty-one-hour drive down and a twenty-one-hour drive back. I timed my order of my CDs just right so I received them on Wednesday for our Friday departure. I didn't want to cut it too close, and yet I didn't want to have a huge $800 bill on my credit card for too long without putting the stuff to use. I got a portable CD player, and while my wife took care of the kids in the back of the van, I listened to Carleton Sheets the whole way down and the whole way back.

Well, with this info in my head, I hit the streets as soon as we returned and looked, called, analyzed everything I could find. I called on over one hundred properties to find the one.

Here's what happened: Within thirty days I had my first property under contract! This property was no ordinary property—it was a commercial strip mall. Facing my fears, I did it anyway. And that one property lead to another and another which then lead to other opportunities that led me here, now an author, speaker, trainer, coach—The Maverick Millionaire®. It seems I had the formula for success: deep desire, great support, quality education, and massive action.

Since then I have gone on to do millions of dollars in real estate, and I now find passion in coaching others to build their dream life by teaching them to "do it different." I decided so many years ago to take a different path and in turn created an abundant life.

IF I can create abundance with a job, a wife, and six kids under six, anyone can do it!

Time to get busy with your journey!

Paul Finck, The Maverick Millionaire®, coaches entrepreneurs and small to midsize companies how to double their results today. With a vast array of knowledge and skill sets from thirty-one-plus years of sales, marketing, and entrepreneurial life experience, Paul dared to be different—he dared to be a maverick. His successes include moving multimillions of dollars in real estate and over $30 million in informational products in the last ten years. Paul Finck's personal life is just as amazing. As a husband and father of three sets of twins, he also knows how to keep life in balance and perspective.

www.TheMaverickDifference.com

HOW I OVERCAME FEAR TO
ACHIEVE SUCCESS AND HAPPINESS

Linda Fleischmann

I had worked in banking for over thirteen years, and after the multiple mergers in the industry, I decided to move to a new profession. I had had some experience with mortgage loans, so I ended up at a mortgage company that did subprime loans. After three months with them, I was laid off and decided to become self-employed.

I started my own company and had my former assistant manager as my partner. After six years of working with her, I found I was bringing in 90 percent of the revenue and she was getting half of the income. So I decided to end that partnership—but ended up with another partner.

What I was missing was that I was fearful of being alone and running a business by myself. At that time, we had ten loan officers, two processors, and an assistant. I was running both the business end of the company as well as bringing in 75 percent of the loans. But I was afraid of doing this alone, without a partner to discuss the different issues that arose. My husband, Mark, is a business consultant and CFO and has extensive knowledge in all areas of business. As he saw me struggling with the business, he saw what I couldn't. I was relying on people that were never going to be there for me, and I was paying for friendship.

As the financial markets were decimated in 2007, the mortgage industry fell apart. I was forced to downsize and move to a smaller location with just my partner and a few loan officers.

During that time, no matter the amount of loans that I closed, I was not getting paid. All of the income was put back into the company. In 2006, the company with over ten loan officers closed 53 million dollars total, and of that, I closed loans totaling 24 million dollars.

In 2008, my partner was working as our processor, and we didn't have any staff. I was able to close 17 million dollars myself, but by 2009, I took home in pay a total of $2,000 for the year.

In 2010, I was networking and got very involved in a women's group where we had monthly speakers. I had heard many speakers, all interesting, but there was only one that seemed to speak to me, and he was talking about writing a book in thirty days.

I had *never* had any desire to write a book, but that seemed to make sense to me. Talk about what you know, and you become an expert in that field by writing a book. So I wrote a book called *How to Have a Stress Free Mortgage, Insider Tips from a Certified Mortgage Broker to Help Save You Time, Money and Frustration.* That was a real accomplishment and made me feel like I was giving back.

These were very difficult years in the mortgage industry with many changes, and having to worry about compliance, administration and employees, along with closing the loans, was very stressful.

My partner had married and had a baby as well. Her hours became nine to five, and mine were seven to seven most days to try to keep up with the volume. My husband kept telling me that I should be on my own, but I was still held captive by the fear of being alone. The other part that kept me from doing anything was that this was MY company; I had built it from nothing. We had a great reputation in the city I was in, and I couldn't fathom not having the company I had built. This was about emotion, not logic, and it was hard to overcome the feelings.

But with the many changes the industry was facing, I started to think more and more about what it would be like to just do loans and not have to manage the company and the people.

We all have our place to where we get pushed and finally go over the edge, and in November of 2010, that point came. My partner had been invited to go to see "Ellen" with the other loan officer in the company. That morning, she came in early for once, at 7:00 a.m. instead of 9:00 since she was leaving at 11:00. I had a lot of loans I was working on, but since she was processing them, when she was gone, I had to do the processing as well. So, as I was in her office going over a few things, I was feeling the stress building and my anger as well.

I asked her if she had to go to see Ellen, and her reply was she didn't have to, but she wanted to . . . and in my head, I thought, "and I want to close loans." All my emotions came out and something inside snapped, and I was finally done. Done with her, done with the company, done with working for everyone—but me.

She came to me a few days later apologizing for the mistakes she had been making, and although I hadn't planned on it, I told her I was done. She looked at me confused and said, done? I said, yes, I'm closing the company and going on my own. And that was it. I finally got over my fear and did what I should have done years before.

In January of 2011, I took a few of the employees we had, closed Loan Connectors, and started my own company called Stress Free Mortgage.

It was the best decision I had ever made. In 2013, I closed 47 million dollars in loans, more loans than I had ever done in the past. The company my license is with takes care of all of the compliance and administration, and I have never been happier or more successful. Overcoming fear is difficult to do, but closing the company I built after thirteen years was the right thing to do.

I have great people working for me, and I have my husband, Mark, who is the only partner I will ever have, both in business and life. That is my success and I am happy, financially strong, and doing what I was meant to do.

Linda Fleischmann started her company in the mortgage industry in 1999 and has helped thousands of clients both purchase homes and refinance their loans. Linda prides herself on her reputation as being able to get her loans closed with the least amount of stress for her clients.

www.StressFreeMortgage.com

TRAIL OF TEARS

Patricia Karen Gagic

The planet earth is expansive, and we are sometimes called to places so distant and remote that we hold our breath and simply believe in the magic of the universe. In 2006 I experienced one such phenomena. My friend Kathy was visiting the sacred temples of Angkor Wat in Siem Reap, Cambodia. During her remarkable tour of the sacred grounds, she ventured off the beaten path through the jungle to the South Pagoda. The fantastic Khmer architecture held her spellbound, as the mysteries seemed to be alive and thriving hundreds of years later. In her vision something quite unusual and caught her attention; it was a large blue sign which read "Orphanage and School for Poor Children" in front of a deteriorated building without a solid roof. There she watched a young boy organizing his blanket under the beams. She was so intrigued that she began a conversation. To her surprise he spoke some English and shared with her the story of the monk who lived there, caring for the children and teaching them on a daily basis. His name is Master Keo Ann.

Captivated by the story and surroundings, she asked many questions as they walked around the compound. Her eyes immediately fell upon a newly poured cement pad with exposed beams. How out of place this seemed amidst the war-torn buildings and stupas in the cemetery. The young boy revealed that Master Keo Ann had a vision to build a library which would serve to preserve the Cambodian folklore and Buddhist teachings which had been buried underground during the time of the Khmer Rouge and were now being rewritten for the future. Kathy listened carefully to the details and decided to call me! Without taking a breath, she said, "Patricia, your name is all over this."

Eight months later, my husband and I completed the library, and in 2007 good fortune allowed us to travel to China and Cambodia. As my feet touched the sacred and mystical soil of Angkor Wat, I could sense the unknown. There were strong feelings of a spiritual awakening along with a deep sadness, remembering the atrocities from thirty years earlier during the time of the Khmer

105

Rouge insurgencies. This was a beautiful nation in need of much support and love combined with a rebirthing of knowledge.

Our visit to the library and meetings with Master Keo Ann stirred a deep karmic connection, as his visions for sustainability of the folklore and Buddhist teachings were now becoming part of my heart and mind. As soon as we returned to Canada, I wrote to Master Keo Ann, asking for his "wish list." What if we could raise enough money to rebuild the school, meeting room, and sleeping quarters and build washrooms and showers? There was much need, and this vision could not be ignored. With the generous help of the Colours of Freedom Foundation, several wonderful friends, and our own personal efforts, we began the renovation and rebuild. It was a miracle. Life for Master Keo Ann and the monks and children now had turned a corner.

The impetus was steady, and next we ventured into building a school for the monks. Master Keo Ann is now recognized as an important teacher and leader in Cambodia, but to me he is an angel with a hero's heart. The small children who lived alone with the monkeys in the jungle now have a place to call home, and the monks now have a teaching school for Buddhist studies.

The impact of the Khmer Rouge left so many people scarred emotionally and physically. Families were torn apart, and many suffered horrific loss. It is time for a healing of the land. Master Keo Ann invited several other districts to a three-day retreat at Ankgor Wat. Over three hundred monks and many nuns and children came to pray and share their stories and respect for all who had lost their lives. The ground was filled with tears. Much of this event was recorded, and the healing could be felt across the earth. It was felt in my heart.

Master Keo Ann became aware of another small village named Boeng Mealea twenty kilometers outside of Siem Reap with a population of 525, comprised of 119 families and 125 children. There is no school or library in this village. Once again our heartstrings were pulled, and a new project is underway to bring education, support, and sustainability of Cambodian folklore and history to the villagers.

The incredible gifts of friendship and love are what make me believe in the power of miracles. There are many lessons I have learned while working with Master Keo Ann over the past decade. The first is to know your own nature and work within its ever-changing boundaries. The second is to trust your instincts and believe that all things are possible with pure intention.

We are one humanity all working to survive with the same consciousness, physical needs, and systems. Striving for excellence regardless of your circumstances opens the door to a plethora of opportunities that can be seen with clarity and compassion.

While the sun and moon are dancing around the elements, we are in control of our destiny. Choices we make become the antidote to the fears we let milk inside us. Release the pressure from within, and you will begin to serve with transparency, authenticity, and accountability. Give yourself permission to remove negative energies from your thoughts and lighten your burdens.

Never has there been a greater time on earth for us to pay attention to our actions. It is a global world. Let us learn to live with a morality which serves one people. When we re-humanize our attitude, we gain expedient wisdom that allows us to cultivate living with a pure heart and mind. Integrity will be your protector and compassion the common expression of your being.

The "Trail of Tears" now flows with happiness and joy.

Patricia Karen Gagic is an international contemporary artist and award-winning author of *Karmic Alibi* and *Karma and Cash*. She was recognized by WXN Women's Executive Network as one of the Top 100 Most Powerful Women in Canada in 2015 and 2016. She was knighted by the International Order of St. George in 2013 and is the recipient of many awards including one from the Canadian Civil Liberties Association in 2017. She is a graduate of the University of Toronto, Faculty of Social Work, a Feng Shui consultant, and a member of the Ontario Cabinet for Friends of the Canadian Museum for Human Rights and The Sir Edmund Hilary Foundation.

www.InspiredToBeRewired.com

bad results. But if you stay on the path of growth, you will see that, as I stated at the beginning, God created all things.

I am still reminded of my mentor Zig Ziglar's last advice to me, telling me I needed to be me. It took a man like Zig to tell me I was great the way I was for me to finally look in the mirror and agree.

I now do the same thing for all those coaches who are part of my blogging classes; you must find out who and what matters to you. That is what you build your blog from; that is the example you teach from.

So, in the end, I found out rock 'n' roll was the tool that mattered to me. God gave me the tool, and He gives me the wisdom to help others with it.

Tim Gillette started with an online blog in 2010 that focused on his love for music, motorcycles, and business mentorship. The blog became a great success and launch tool for his speaking and coaching business. Now Tim uses the same tools to create his Rock Around Your Blog system to help coaches and speakers build a blog to help them stand out online.

www.NotTomPetty.com

STAND UP AND SPEAK UP

Walt Grassl

If you're not going to speak up, how is the world
supposed to know you exist?
—Author Unknown

In 2006, I had been working for a Fortune 500 company for over 30 years. I had advanced from test technician to Senior Engineering Manager. I led a department of 100 engineers. It looked like I was having a great career. But looks can be deceiving.

Annual performance reviews were consistently outstanding. Yet, there was a consistent opportunity for improvement—my communication skills.

Why? I suffered from leg shaking, hand shaking, perspiration dripping, dry mouth, mind going blank stage fright.

Stage fright appeared when presenting to peers, management, and customers. It also appeared in interviews for higher-level positions. Had I addressed stage fright earlier in my career, I would have risen higher and faster within the company.

In 2006, I had to deliver a critically important message to a group of our employees. My boss was in the audience and observed my less than stellar delivery. He called me into his office and told me I could no longer ignore the issue. He sent me to our HR manager to figure out a way to fix me, and he suggested I join the Toastmasters club at our facility.

I reluctantly joined Toastmasters, and my initial progress was slow. I only spoke six times in the first 18 months. Joining a group will not make you better. You have to do the work.

While I did not speak a lot, I attended Toastmasters speech contests to watch good speakers. In October 2007, I spoke to the keynote speaker at our District Conference before he gave his speech. I decided to invest in myself by purchasing his training materials.

In February of 2008, I made a bigger investment. I attended three speaker-training events in Las Vegas: Storytelling, Humor, and a general speaking seminar called Lady & the Champs.

During the humor seminar, I got up on stage to deliver a two-line joke I had just written a few minutes before. My mind went blank. I picked up my notes. My hands were shaking so bad, I had a hard time reading the joke. At the end of the event, I was frustrated to tears. It was suggested I try an open mic night. "If you get in front of a crowd and get even one laugh, you will learn to relax. Don't compare yourself to people who are at the top of their game. Look at others who are just starting out." Right!

At Lady & the Champs, I talked to attendees and presenters. I asked how they overcame stage fright. Nothing resonated with me. But I noticed that these speakers were NOT dripping with charisma. They were just like me, without the fear.

On the flight back home, I realized I had a long journey ahead of me, but I was determined to conquer stage fright. I set the goal of being good enough to get paid to speak by August of 2012, when I would be 55 and old enough to retire.

I vowed to speak at my Toastmasters club at least once a month. I joined three more clubs. I committed to speaking in all available Toastmaster speech contests. It was difficult at first, but the more I spoke, the easier it got. Repetition builds confidence.

At one of the contests, I heard about improv, which is unscripted comedy. I found a class and signed up. In improv, I struggled at first, trying to plan ahead and not being present in the moment. I learned to listen and trust that I could pull something out of my head to move the scene forward.

Next, I enrolled in a standup comedy class. I put together a five-minute comedy set to perform at the Hollywood Improv. Yikes!

On a Sunday night in March of 2009, I was at the Hollywood Improv. The show was open to the public. Two hundred people were well into their two-drink minimum. I thought, "What am I doing here?"

I was scared witless . . . literally. You see, halfway through my set, my mind blanked. I pulled my joke list out of my pocket, looked at it and put it back. Then I forgot what I had just read. I slowly pulled it out again, got a laugh and then finished my set.

I got laughs! I went from sheer terror to the most exhilarating moment of my life. What a rush.

After that, speaking in front of 200 sober Toastmasters was nothing. Ok, I was still scared—but much less so. Speaking at work was a piece of cake. Over time, I even performed in local improv and sketch comedy shows.

As August of 2012 approached, I felt I was good enough to get paid to speak. But, how? I joined a MasterMind group. I shared my story of overcoming stage fright and my MasterMind peers helped me develop Stand Up & Speak Up. They inspired me to host a radio show, write a book, and audition to get into the prestigious Groundlings School for improv and sketch comedy.

In February of 2015, I was at Lady & the Champs again. As I took my seat, the gentleman next to me said, "Are you Walt Grassl?"

He went on to say he was at the event because he heard about it on my radio show. He said he listened to the podcasts regularly. He found out about it in a Google search.

Wow. I was floored. Up until now, I thought only friends or friends of guests listened to the show. I felt like a "RockStar."

I began this incredible journey to face a fear and improve my career. Over time, I decided to encourage other people to overcome their fears. To learn that people are finding me and that I am making a difference just feels so good.

When will you stand up and speak up, and let the world know you exist?

———————

Walt Grassl is a professional speaker, author, radio personality, and entertainer. Walt delivers his leadership message "Good Leaders Ask Dumb Questions" to corporate, collegiate, and conference audiences.

www.WaltGrassl.com

What Doesn't Kill You
Makes You Stronger

Darrell Griffin

M y mom, Shirley, met and married my dad, David "Ross" Griffin, in Rodeo, California. He was your typical punk—an eighteen-year-old kid that hung out on the corner, collar turned up, sunglasses and a toothpick hanging from his mouth. Ross soon became a member of the Hells Angels. His family was so proud of him.

One late night in 1956, my mom hitched a ride home with her boss from the bar where she was a hostess. Her boss had had too much to drink and lost control of the car, hitting a telephone pole. Shirley left behind four children, one-year-old Sandra, two-year-old Sharon, three-year-old Sheila, and me—four-year-old Darrell.

We went to live with our Grandpa and Grandma Moxley. Grandpa was not able to work due to crippling arthritis. Grandma had to find a job as a cook's helper at a school in Stockton, California. My sisters and I had to work with Grandma and Grandpa picking walnuts in the mornings and weekends. I remember going to my first day of second grade with my hands stained dark brown from picking walnuts. I was so embarrassed. I walked around school all day with my hands in my pockets, hoping no one would notice.

At fourteen Grandma found me a job at the Rare Steer restaurant where she was now working. Between the welfare checks, Grandma's fry cook wages, and my dishwasher earnings, we got by.

Grandpa and I did not get along very well much of the time. A lot of it was due to my sixteen-year-old attitude; I felt I knew everything. I remember one of the last arguments I had with my grandpa. The welfare caseworker told him about a typewriter repair center at the downtown Stockton Vocational Center.

"Skip," Grandpa said to me, "I want you to get into that typewriter repair program. You ain't college material. There will always be typewriters, so you will always have a job."

Well, I am glad I did not become a typewriter repairman. I was right on this one. The straw that broke the camel's back with Grandpa was when he found out my girlfriend was pregnant. There I was—sixteen, in high school, a dad, a dishwasher, living in a dusty trailer park. Not too promising of a future at this point, but I was about to meet one of the many "angels" in my life.

I was going to high school full-time and working full-time, and I was barely making it. Then I lost my job. I remember asking God if he could spread the bad luck around a little more.

I heard that the Hoosier Inn, owned by Charles Dyer, was looking for dishwashers. It was the "go-to" place for families after church and truckers during the week. I stopped by and was hired right away. I will always remember the famous quotes over every door and on every cross beam:

Success is 10 percent inspiration and 90 percent perspiration. (Thomas Edison)

Do the same thing you have always done, and you will get what you have always got. (Anonymous)

Good things come to people who wait, but better things come to those who go out and get them. (Anonymous)

Just when the caterpillar thought the world was ending, he turned into a butterfly. (Proverb)

I have not failed. I have just found 10,000 ways that won't work. (Thomas Edison)

If you are going through hell, keep going. —Winston Churchill

I find that the harder I work, the more luck I seem to have. (Thomas Jefferson)

Choose a job you love, and you will never have to work a day in your life. (Confucius)

Mr. Dyer found out that I could not afford my books and tuition. Coincidentally, my split of the daily tips shot up so that it covered my books and tuition. I am sure it was Mr. Dyer's doing. Coincidence is God's way of remaining anonymous.

I had been less than a "C" student in middle school and high school. Living on my own must have agreed with me because in my senior year I earned all "As." I was the first in my family to graduate from high school. I didn't want to do what the other men in my family did. I didn't want to work at the local cereal factory or coat hanger factory, and I didn't want to drive a truck. I didn't want to work until the whistle blew, then spend the evening drinking a countless number of six packs. I knew there was more to life, and I wanted it. I decided I had to change course. The Hoosier Inn quotes motivated me.

After high school, I got a job at a paint store, the Paul Cox Studio. I remember being amazed at the homes in the area. All of them had lawns that covered their front yards and no one parked cars on the grass. Paul was another "angel." He would purposely schedule my hours when no customers were in the store. When the store was empty, he encouraged me to work on my homework. With his help, I was able to support my family and graduate college.

After college I became a controller at Foster Farms, one of the largest poultry companies in America. While at Foster Farms I obtained a master's degree, with a 4.00 GPA from my alma mater, Stanislaus. This is where I met Kim, my wife of thirty-five years. Kim would help me raise my two oldest children. We had a total of six beautiful children between us.

Tragedy struck again in 2007. Our oldest son Skip, who had joined the Army, was deployed to Iraq. He was killed by a sniper in Baghdad. To finish a book we were working on, I traveled to Iraq and embedded with his combat unit. I finished our book, *Last Journey*, in 2009. Kim and I would not have been able to get through this ordeal without our faith in God. "Now faith is confidence in what we hope for and assurance about what we do not see" (Hebrews 11:1).

Our faith would be tested again a few years later. I was diagnosed with a tumor on my pituitary gland. When they did a post-surgery MRI and examination, they determined I had MS.

We have had our ups and downs—thankfully more ups than downs. We learned that:

- God will guide you if you listen to him.
- Hard work does pay off.
- Be willing to change directions.
- You are not defeated unless you say you are.

I still remember the quotes from the Hoosier Inn.

Darrell Griffin, MBA, CPA, is a small business consultant and a writer. He and his wife, Kim, who is also a CPA, run the online bookstore www.quickeasyreads.com. It's motto—"We are ODD—One who Dares to be Different. Embracing diversity one short book at time"—is a reflection of Kim and Darrell's approach to life. Kim graduated from UCLA with a degree in Economics and Darrell graduated from California State University, Stanislaus, with an MBA with a 4.00 GPA. Darrell is the author of *Last Journey* that is based on his embed with his son's combat unit in Baghdad after his son was killed in combat. *God Think* is the title of his next book.

THIS IS ONLY A TEST

Terri Hardin

There she is . . . God's little dandy-lion. As a little girl the first thing you saw when you looked at me was my hair, just like today. Back then it was a curse, and today it's my trademark. It's funny how things work out.

In a little town in California, my white mother took one look at my black father, and they fell instantly in love. This was 1956, the same time Rosa Parks was fighting for her seat on the bus. They wanted to get married, but the state didn't allow it, so they had to go to Mexico.

One year later I was born. A little baby, white as snow with a lion's mane of golden blonde hair that stuck out in all directions.

So much frizzy hair! How will I take care of it? she thought.

This wasn't our only challenge.

When you were little, do you remember your mom or dad escorting you to the bathroom? My skin was so light and my father's so dark, he couldn't take me to the bathroom because there were separate bathrooms—one for whites and one for blacks. Imagine if my father had taken me inside the way so many parents of the same color did over and over without giving it a second thought.

My father would've been arrested.

One time I went to get a drink of water with my father. As I walked to the fountain he was drinking from, he stopped me. Shaking his head, he directed me to the white drinking fountain. I couldn't drink next to my daddy like other kids, and I just didn't understand.

My parents tried to explain, but this made no sense to me.

The real trouble began with I started going to school. My looks made me a prime target of bullies. I was constantly cornered by small bands of snarling kids pulling my hair and calling me names like "Bozo" or "Phyllis Diller." If I stood up to them or tried not to react, they would punch me and try to beat me up. I held my own pretty well, but it hurt to be so alone. One time someone threw a match in my hair, and it burst into flame. Thank goodness the two friends I did have had fast hands that put out the fire before it got bad.

My second grade teacher refused to call me by my name. On the first day of class, she began to call roll. When she got to my name, she glared down at me and snarled, "Black Sambo." I thought she had made a mistake, so I corrected her. "I'm Terri," I said. Drawing her face closer, she repeated sternly, "Oh no, it's Black Sambo!"

Shocked, my parents went to the principal who told them nothing could be done as this teacher had tenure. This was my life.

One afternoon, after a long day of humiliation at school, I came home, my clothes all disheveled and dirty having scrapped with the usual ill-mannered kids. Exhausted and feeling like I had fought for my very life, I collapsed in a heap on the front stoop. I buried my head in my hands and began to cry.

I didn't notice my father arriving home from work. Seeing that I was upset, he looked down and asked, "Something wrong?"

I looked up, my face dirty, and my eyes red from crying. "Oh, Dad! Why can't my hair be like Mary Tyler Moore's, swooping down with that cute little flip like everybody else's?" I sobbed.

My father sighed and sat next to me on the stoop. "You need to take a deep breath and close your eyes."

"Aw, Dad, this is serious! I don't have time to close my eyeeeees!"

"Terri, sweetheart, calm down and close your eyes."

With a deep sigh of resignation, I closed my eyes. My father paused and then asked me to imagine a beautiful rose.

"Have you got it? What does it look like?"

"It's pink with dark pink edges."

I didn't see the point, but this *was* my favorite kind of rose.

Dad then asked me to imagine my rose surrounded by a huge field of weeds—nothing but weeds as far as the eye could see. The weeds filled my vision, and only one rose stood in the middle of all of them . . . my rose.

"Do you see all of those weeds?"

"Yes, Daddy."

"Do you see the rose?"

"Yes, Daddy."

"Okay, now I want you to ask yourself this question. Do you really want to be a weed, like everyone else, like the masses you see? Or would you rather be the rose?"

Silence . . .

Suddenly my eyes flew open, and I looked up at my father in wonder.

"You are unique, Terri, like the rose, and being unique is never easy. It's very special, and it takes courage to be unique. You have to decide if you're up to this task, as greatness doesn't come to everyone. You are different, so embrace it."

This story changed me. The bullies, I decided, were there to test me. If I could survive them, I was destined for greatness. We must often prove we're worthy by defeating life's tests and rising above the ashes like a phoenix.

If we just give up, complain, and don't defeat these tests, we may never experience the greatness we deserve. We must pick ourselves up, dust ourselves off, and just keep swimming, as Dory says in *Finding Nemo*. Again and again, no matter what it takes.

Movement in any direction creates momentum, even if the direction is the wrong one. The key is to move and never ever give up.

Today I'm an international success as an artist. I'm known as Walt Disney's Legendary Imagineer, having designed attractions all over the world. I'm a Jim Henson Puppeteer, and I've appeared in over forty-eight TV shows and films, including *Ghostbusters*. I speak all over the world on how to make a living doing what you love and the importance of collaboration. I inspire others to fight for their dreams.

I design and create custom art and prototypes for individuals and corporations along with teaching classes and mentoring.

It wasn't easy, and it's good to remember that there are some people whose dream is to steal yours. But if you're willing to fight for your dreams and not simply believe in them, then this is only a test, and you will rise victorious.

Never give up, and remember that you're unique and you deserve complete success. Are you up to the task?

Terri Hardin, known as Walt Disney's Legendary Imagineer, is responsible for creating Disneyland Paris's Big Thunder Mountain and the Dragon's Lair attractions and the Splash Mountain attraction in Tokyo. Her company, Terri Hardin Designs, Inc., sculpts prototypes and custom artwork for anyone needing someone to turn their vision into reality. A world-renowned artist, author, Henson Puppeteer, and International speaker, Terri tours all over the world sharing her stories of imagineering and working with Jim Henson, encouraging others to strive to work at what they love to earn a living. Other credits include *Ghostbusters, Men in Black,* and *Dinosaurs.*

www.TerriHardinSpeaks.com

Triumph Over Tragedy

Linda Hodge

At some point in our lives, we encounter challenging or tragic circumstances. For countless people, it's the loss of a parent or child that creates a painful void where alcohol, drugs, and sex become the "welcome" panacea. Others may experience a life-threatening accident or illness, which often leaves them "drowning" in hopelessness. Oftentimes survivors of unspeakable childhood circumstances carry emotional scars, leaving them psychologically debilitated. For myself, I endured years of both physical and emotional abuse at the hands of my first husband, "Joe."

Getting married at eighteen years of age was one of the worst mistakes of my life. Marrying an abusive, overly controlling alcoholic only added fuel to the fire. Joe was this super-macho type, which I found very enticing and challenging. He made me feel safe, especially since my dad had passed away when I was twelve. Consequently, I grew up looking for a protector and hero. Joe carried guns, sold weed, and drank beer all day. He was a womanizer who never held down a job longer than a month. What's more, the verbal abuse Joe inflicted toward his mom should've been a red flag, indicating a potentially dangerous future.

For the next seven years, my life rotated on a sphere of continual chaos. The physical abuse started shortly after we married. A guy asked me to dance at a local nightclub, and I agreed. Immediately upon leaving the dance floor, Joe hurriedly rushed me outside the building. Enraged, he began calling me every degrading name one could imagine. Upon arriving at his mom's home, Joe forced me into the bedroom, where the true torture began. One after another, Joe continued slapping and punching me.

I only seemed to make the situation worse by trying to defend myself. I knew Joe had the upper hand, so I didn't fight mightily. All the while, I was hoping his mom would rescue me at any moment. That never happened. She didn't appear until the gun went off. After reaching for a gun, Joe pointed it directly toward my face. I heard a shot and was paralyzed from intense fear. My heart was beating fast and erratically. A lump rose in my throat. I didn't know if I had survived the shot.

Shortly thereafter I realized the bullet had just missed my head. But my skull was throbbing. While on the bed dodging the gun, I had hit the back of my head on the window pane. I was seeing stars and crying out to God.

The remaining years of my marriage didn't get any better as I was becoming more enabled and made to feel like a fool. I felt worthless and helpless. Yet I was caught between having the desire for my marriage to succeed and an awareness that my life could possibly end. The price tag of remaining in that relationship outweighed the need for love.

Eventually I got the strength to say "So long!" to pain.

Usually, at one time or another while growing up, a child's crayon may break while coloring. Some may decide to no longer color, while others choose to use the broken crayon. The latter group knows the broken crayon still works! Therefore they continue coloring their picture. Many lives have been broken from choices people made or situations that happened to them. Subsequently they choose to no longer color their picture. Even with a broken life, you can repair it and move forward coloring your world! Pick back up your dreams and begin to place texture and purpose into your life. I possessed a story my past needed to tell my present. It was time to rewrite the script of my life.

Prior to embarking on this journey I needed to answer a few questions: "Why do you feel that you are not good enough? Why settle for average? Why not remove limits and break the chains of self-defeating behaviors? Why is it difficult to love yourself?

Being physically free from a volatile environment doesn't necessarily mean you are emotionally or mentally free. Mental prisons are like invisible walls secretly lurking—afraid of being identified and detected. But on one quiet morning, honesty began to speak within the corridors of my soul. Her voice heightened and hushed the pretentious world I had created. Face-to-face, I was confronted with honesty. There wasn't enough makeup or concealer to hide my damaged soul.

Honesty took me by the hand and assured me that she could relieve my pain. Honesty didn't abuse me. She wanted to heal me. Honesty assured me that if I held tightly, I would never have to live again in denial. It was time for me to emerge. It wasn't an easy task. But daily I trained my willpower not to be governed by personal emotions. I made affirmations for what I couldn't see within myself but was in expectation of improving. "I am loved, accepted, needed by myself and others." This exercise caused me to adjust my thought and communication. "Belief and speech" were the keys to a new lease on life.

After I became acquainted with honesty, I was introduced to "courage." Fear was a shadow moving with every step I attempted to make. Inevitably I was incapable of being courageous when making decisions. Fear of making wrong choices led to fear of making myself a priority. Inadequacy feelings tortured and silenced me when my voice needed to be heard. Feelings of condemnation directly assaulted my faith. It was also an enemy to my confidence in God and me. Condemnation was causing me to shrink back. Instead of feeling worthy, I felt ashamed and lacked boldness. Feelings of mental anguish, anxiety, and self-doubt caused me to become "intoxicated" with images of being stuck in misery. I came to realize that failure is an inside job.

Transformation requires changing doubt into belief and fear into faith! Remaining the same produces the same results. In order to fully grasp my future, I had to release my past: no longer dwelling on horrible mistakes and abusive relationship choices. It was time to reach for my future through "expectation." There was more for me than I had previously experienced. I needed the perseverance to rewrite the script of my life.

I survived because the fire inside me burned brighter than the fire around me. As a survivor of numerous obstacles, I've learned what it takes to "triumph over tragedy."

———————————

Linda Hodge works with women who have repeated patterns of self-sabotage that cause frustration, limited beliefs, and problematic behaviors. As a result of her tools and systems, clients minimize their tendency to revert to prior habits, and break through self-imposed limitations. Those who practice her methods not only experience external behavior changes, but also transform their internal thought processes. Since utilizing her coaching services, countless women attest to living the quality of life they desire and deserve.

The author of five books, Linda and her husband, Dr. Fred L. Hodge Jr., are the founders of Transformation Mentoring Culture, which provides workshops and e-Lessons.

www.LindaGHodge.com

Free Falling

Deborah Kagan

I thought for sure I'd lost my mind as I lay prostrate, face down on my kitchen floor. It was 1997. A lovely summer day in West Hollywood, California. The birds were singing, the sun was shining, and everything seemed to click along normally . . . except in my kitchen.

Moments prior I had been standing in my robe making a tea latte. Next thing I know, I got bitch-slapped really, really hard on the back of my neck. So hard I wound up on the floor. That might all make sense if there was an actual other person in my apartment. Alas, just me. Here's where it gets even more "Twilight Zone-y." I heard whispering. Like the whispers in the TV from "Poltergeist." They don't make sense at first. It's when you shout back at them saying, WHAT?! I hear you. But what-are-you-saying?! That's when they press pause on the static button, part the energy field, and say three words in one very eerie, albeit clear voice: Light. Love. Truth. And whoosh. Whatever was there exited the building like it was late for lunch with a lover.

That shove from above, as I've come to call it, changed my life. I had been teetering with keeping my career in the film business, you know, to have something to fall back on, while at the same time I was starting a Feng Shui consulting business.

As much as I tried to ignore the shove for a few days, it lingered. I could feel it leaning on me in the shower. I could feel it sitting shotgun in my car giving me googly eyes. I could feel it spooning with me in bed. Until I finally couldn't ignore it anymore.

Fine! I huffed. *What now?*

Before I knew it, I found myself walking into the Bodhi Tree Bookstore, THE new age mecca in Los Angeles. I loved wandering around in there. Fabulous people-watching. A bazillion books to peruse. Groovy crystal-y things to ogle.

Wandering towards the astrology aisle, a pretty blonde, cut straight from a JC Penny catalog, sat pouring over the book *Lovesigns*, while a 40-something soccer mom stood wistfully reading pages from a Rumi poetry book.

I found myself in the symbols/symbolism section. A thin, orange book literally fell off the shelf by my feet. Being on this quest to pay attention to these new, persistent messages, I picked up the book and read the title, *The Book of Signs* (how's that for on the nose?). I flipped through the first few pages, and there they were. Triangles. Big deal you might be thinking. A geometric symbol used in math and science. Whoopdeedo. Here's where it gets freaky. A right-side-up triangle represents Light. The Masculine. An upside-down triangle represents Truth. The Feminine. Put the two of them together, and you get Love. A beautiful union of the masculine and feminine. The complete picture of what's so in the universe, and the message that had originally knocked me down. That's when I knew synchronicity exists. For reals.

Some people get cancer. Some car accidents. Some lose a loved one. I got the psychic slap to fall down in order to soar. I had no idea exactly how it would go. What I did know was to pay closer attention to the whispers, let instincts be the guide, see where it leads, and allow my life to change. What you are meant to learn and experience falls into your life, the question is how to take the opportunity and recalibrate.

Since that oh-so-wild morning in my sweet Spanish bungalow of an apartment, I have built a thriving Feng Shui consulting business working in private homes, corporate offices, Hollywood film sets, hotels, and even a casino in Vegas. Atma Jewels, a complimentary product line, was birthed in 2000, making headlines in numerous publications, and was featured in a celebrity-gifting suite.

The year 2008 ushered in the next big shove from above. This time it was way friendlier. I was in New Orleans at the Superdome for the tenth anniversary of VDAY, a global organization dedicated to ending violence against women. I wasn't even three feet inside when the voice from above fell into my brain.

"Hey, Deborah. It's time to get up off your ass and do the work with women."

I could feel my body falling forward into the YES of the message, which is a distinctly different feeling than tipping back into a NO.

"I don't know what you want me to do. But I'm listening," I replied.

Nearly nine years later, from the humble beginnings of hosting women's circles in my living room to stages speaking to as many as a thousand at a time, I've had the pleasure of working with over 10,000 women, in person or online, helping them rock their mojo. Plus, I've had the honor of producing two events featuring Calista Flockhart, Rosario Dawson, Dylan McDermott, Christine Lahti, and others where we raised money and awareness for VDAY, a cause close to my heart.

Some people's RockStar moment hits them bluntly over the head. For most of us, it's much more subtle. It's an idea or thought or feeling that haunts you and lingers. Start paying attention to that and take actions congruent with the message.

My entrée to being an entrepreneur came from a psychic bitch-slap to the neck. Normal? I'd say not. Fits the trend for my life, though, as I've never been much of a conventional one. Which works to my benefit as an entrepreneur. Because when you're out to blaze a trail, make a mark, or share your gift with the world, it's better if you can play on the edge.

And hey, when we have the pleasure to meet, remind me to show you how I made an indelible mark to remember that moment, the one that allowed me to get up off the floor and create a life worth living.

―――――――――

Deborah Kagan helps women rock their mojo. She is the creator of the Rock Your Mojo™ programs and the author of "Find Your ME Spot: 52 Ways to Reclaim Your Confidence, Feel Good in Your Own Skin and Live a Turned On Life."

For all things mojolicious, check out
www.Deborah-Kagan.com.

IGNITE YOUR SPEAKING POWER

Melody Keymer Harper

There we were, my twin sister, Marilyn, and I, ten years old, standing in the middle of the auditorium stage with a microphone and hundreds of people sitting in the audience, staring at us, when out of the blue it struck. An intensely uncomfortable feeling I had not experienced before swept over my entire body, settling deep within my stomach and making my knees shake. I will never forget it!

Our other sister, Rochelle, was energetically playing away on the piano, accompanying us as we sang a Maguire Sisters song, "Sugartime," when I experienced my first bout of stage fright.

With our arms wrapped around each other's waist, facing the audience, Marilyn knew exactly what it meant when she felt the prodding pokes I was giving her on her back. We were singing the chorus and the verse was coming up . . . my solo . . . and I suddenly decided there was no way I was going to sing it.

Being very connected as twins, we have always been able to sense what each other is thinking or feeling, and I instantly knew when she poked my back that she had no intention of singing the solo either.

With slightly more urging, I again poked her back, as if to say, "Please help me out." Again she poked me in reply as if to say, "You are the one who sings the melody, I sing the harmony, and it is your solo, so sing it!"

I gave one last, firm insistent poke and decided that if she did not sing the solo, I was going to just stand there clapping my hands, keeping time to the instrumental music until the chorus came back. And, bless her little heart, she pulled it through and sang the solo.

We made it through the rest of the song together and nobody had a clue what was going on between the two of us as we bowed to the sounds of enthusiastic applause.

The question that I hear most, no matter what age group I'm speaking to is, "How and why did you become a professional speaker?" Here is how it all came about . . .

126

When I was three years old, my mom entered my twin sister and me in a talent contest at Crawford's Market, a local farmers market in San Gabriel, the city where I grew up. Wearing short green dresses with white collars and puffy short sleeves, white ankle socks with lace, and shiny little black Mary Jane shoes, we looked like two little "Shirley Temples" with curly brown hair, as we sang in unison to the tune of "I Love You a Bushel and a Peck," the song our mom used to sing to us after reading each night before going to bed.

We won first place, a huge bag of groceries for the family, and instantly fell in love with singing on stage. Mom entered us in numerous contests after that, and we kept winning!

We discovered we really liked showbiz and hearing the applause from people with smiling faces that we seemed to make feel happy from what we were doing.

By the time we were ten, we were getting paid to sing in productions and on radio and TV variety shows. At the age of sixteen, we received our AFTRA union membership when landing the twin lead roles in a pilot for a new TV series called *The Jackson Twins*, with actors Dennis O'Keefe and Jan Clayton playing our parents. This was followed by receiving our SAG union membership from appearing in the movie *Double Trouble* with Elvis Presley and our AEO union membership for performing on stage with Mickey Rooney and Jose Ferrer in *A Funny Thing Happened on the Way to the Forum*.

Elvis Presley, Johnny Carson, and Mickey Rooney were major contributors to helping me overcome my fear of public speaking and being on stage. Did you know that both Elvis Presley and Johnny Carson had stage fright every time they went on stage?

You wouldn't know it to look at them. That is what people say to me as well. I learned from them how to harness the fear and use it to give better performances, which is what I do today in my coaching programs, seminars, and two-day events.

It was important to my parents that, even though I was in the theatrical world, I would be raised like the "girl next door." I went to the local elementary and high schools, sang in the church choir, and participated in school activities, including being on the Pep Squad, singing with the a cappella and swing choirs, acting in Drama Club productions, and being a member of Student Government and the Debate Team.

My bachelor's degree in Psychology and master's degree in Career Development and Community Counseling later afforded me the opportunity to teach and counsel in the corporate, educational, and entrepreneurial sectors.

I had a number of mentors over the years, starting with my parents, Elvis Presley, and Johnny Carson, that helped me learn how to control those butterflies. Everyone needs someone to guide them, no matter what level of expertise they are.

Later I invested in speaking and marketing coaches James Malinchak and

Craig Duswalt. They gave me sound guidance on combining my past experiences in the theatrical world and education to use entertainment and my strong communication skills to teach others how to overcome their fear of public speaking and to convey their compelling message with confidence.

This inspired me to host my *Double Trouble Talk Radio* show with my twin sister on "How to Convey Your Message with Confidence," co-author my first book, *Double Trouble Transformation System for Women: Fast and Easy Strategies to Guide Women in Their Transformation from Parent to Entrepreneur*, and create my Ignite Your Speaking Power program to train people how to overcome their fear of public speaking and deliver their compelling message with confidence to get the winning results they want on stage, in media, in their career, and in life.

Let me ask you a few questions:

- Do your hands get sweaty, your legs start shaking, or do you feel butterflies flying around in the pit of your stomach when you have to stand up and speak in front of an audience?
- Do you sometimes start a sentence and then somehow forget how to finish it?
- Do you miss out on opportunities due to a lack of confidence in communicating?

You are not alone! More than half the population feels the same way. Success in our personal and career lives depend directly on how effective our communication skills are.

Melody Keymer Harper, speaker, author, entertainer, radio host, and creator of Ignite Your Speaking Power, knows what it takes to become a successful speaker. She has over thirty years of experience teaching successful speaking strategies. Melody has designed programs and successfully delivered over two thousand seminars and trainings nationally to thousands of people in all levels of business.

Aside from acting in the movie *Double Trouble* with Elvis Presley, Melody has also appeared with Johnny Carson, Betty White, Mickey Rooney, Debbie Reynolds, and Elizabeth Taylor, and has shared the stage with speaking giants like Jack Canfield, Brian Tracy, Mark Victor Hanson, and Denis Waitley.

www.MelodyKeymerHarper.com

THRIVE—NO MATTER WHAT

Dr. Theodoros Kousouli

Have you struggled in life—more than you think is fair? Have you been beaten down so much that you've asked, "Why me?"

We all experience trials and tribulations, some more than others. I myself, now a successful doctor in Beverly Hills, once believed that I couldn't handle anymore adversity. I was weighed down early in childhood, believing that something was wrong with me. But through my struggles, I learned that life is far more precious when you fight for it.

From kindergarten through grade school, I was often bullied for nothing more than being small in stature and an easy target. As I entered my teens, the bullying intensified; I started to clam up, never sharing myself with anyone, to avoid further humiliation.

Between the beatings in school and the lack of emotional support in my own house, I crawled inside myself—deep inside. I felt that I was ugly, flawed, and unlovable. By age fifteen, the bullying at school became unbearable. To escape, I decided to end my life.

Just as I was about to slice my wrists, a voice inside sternly said, "No!" It echoed through me like thunder, and my grip on the razor went limp. Unexpectedly, divine perception offered me clarity: It was the environment that was sick, not me. All of a sudden, I knew I was here for a reason, and I believed that there was something grander that needed to be done but was yet unfinished. For the first time in my life, I realized that I had more control than I thought—I was who I knew myself to be—a very powerful soul.

During a summer break in Greece, my friends and I played games of "chicken" and, in a round that did not go our way, the partner on my shoulders lost the wrestling match. As he fell, his legs took my head and neck with him. There was a violent snap to the right, and immediately pain sunk deep into my neck and chest. My left arm went weak, my heart and lungs became heavy, and I had difficulty breathing.

Weeks later, I had tried everything: massage, physical therapy, pills—nothing helped. One day I tried a local chiropractor in town. I figured that some "pseu-do-science"—as my father called it—might bring me some relief! In one fast swoop of the doctor's hands as he adjusted my spine, I heard an audible noise as power surged into my body, and I regained full function! I started to gasp at the sensations overtaking me in a rush of relief. The peaceful serenity from the sudden release of pain that I was in brought me to tears.

With total amazement, respect, and gratitude for my miracle, my perception of what true healing was—shifted. I uttered the words that began everything I am today: "Doctor, I want to do this for others, like you did for me." Soon after I registered for chiropractic school, but my life lessons in healing had already started.

I will never forget October 5, 2005. "You have eight months to live if we don't replace your valve. Your heart will burst, and you'll internally bleed to death." It doesn't sink in at first when you're told that you might die soon.

The cardiologist diagnosed cardiomegaly: an enlarged heart due to the stress of pumping blood. My aortic valve had been malformed since birth, and instead of pumping blood away from the heart, it was leaking blood backwards, causing me to black out twice.

I was upset that the only options my cardiologist offered were a metal valve that needed lifetime Coumadin (a blood thinner to keep the valve's metal joints from clotting and causing strokes) or an animal valve that would require another surgery later.

I chose the cow valve, knowing I would face the same fate again when the valve degenerated. However, unlike the metal valve's need for blood thinners, I would at least have a chance at a more normal life.

As I was prepped for surgery, I realized that I'd lived too selfishly and egotistically. I took too much for granted—my family, my friends, my time, my purpose. What a waste to not make something more of the gifts and talents I'd been given. So I prayed, "God, if you want me to come back—and yes, I do want to come back—I will dedicate my time to serving you through helping others. Let me know you are with me, and when people ask for help, let me be able to give it to them through your grace."

The surgery was rough, but I made it. The cardiologist told me that full recovery would take four to six months. Thanks to a combination of prayer, nutrition, self-hypnosis, and chiropractic care, I super healed in only forty-five days post-surgery! This experience led me to develop the Kousouli® Method, my holistic healing program, and many self-help materials for patients.

I knew this experience was defining; it changed me on a fundamental level as a result of my brush with death. Death, however, was not yet finished teaching me.

Eleven years later, the surgery to replace the valve that had been given to me at age twenty-eight came. The old valve was failing, and I also had an aneurysm in my aortic arch. With this second and even more dangerous surgery came all of those same frustrations and concerns: What if I don't make it? What if . . . this is it?

But, because of the practices I'd established through my journey—nutritionally, physically, mentally, and spiritually—the second surgery and my recuperation were easier than the first. Two months after my second valve replacement, I was back to work helping patients heal! Without a radical shift in my perception of healing and the definition of a life well-lived, I wouldn't be here today.

Despite the success, my path was not always clear. I experienced so much adversity and trauma early in life, and yet it molded who I am and where I am today. I grew and changed as I tried to find my own way in a world that was not always kind to me.

You can do it, too, no matter what you've experienced or what you're currently going through. Are you ready to reach your full potential? With the right mentor and support, you can live a full life while overcoming obstacles with grace and love. I've been there. I know you can overcome anything—no matter what.

Dr. Theodoros Kousouli, DC,CHT, is an intuitive mind-body holistic healer with a thriving practice in Beverly Hills, California. Dr. Kousouli does radical life enhancement and transformation for those seeking top performance, personal power, and a pain-free existence. He works with an array of people, from business leaders, CEOs, professional athletes to celebrities and housewives. He helps his patients remove their challenges and find their inner power by reprogramming their mind and body via the nervous system. He has also created The Kousouli® Method, a proprietary combination of chiropractic and hypnosis healing modalities that encourages holistic balance catered to the individual. To become a patient, call (310) 777-3463 or visit www.DrKousouli.com. For live seminar information, please visit www.KousouliMethod.com. For personal empowerment books and materials, please visit www.BeAMaster.com.

www.DrKousouli.com

master's degree, I'm thirty years old and dating a guy whose father passes away suddenly. I'm up very early that next morning to drop my boyfriend at the airport, and when I get back home and can't get back to sleep, I call home. Ironically my dad answers the phone, which he normally doesn't, but my mom is out, so it's him on the line . . .

"Hey kid, whatcha doing up . . . isn't it like 6:00 a.m. out there?"

"Yeah, it is early. I couldn't sleep," I reply. "You remember my boyfriend? Well, his father suddenly died last night. I just dropped him off at the airport." True to form, my dad makes a crack to deflect anything emotional.

"So you're calling to see if your 'old man' is still kicking."

"Yeah," I answer back with a chuckle, "I'm calling to see if you're still kicking, Dad."

"Well, yeah, I'm doing pretty good. My golf game could use some help, but being retired I guess I've got plenty of time to work on it. So it's not so bad."

We talk a bit more about nothing terribly important: I fill him in on other things going on in my life, and he tells me a little bit about the garden my mom is planting. We chat for a little while longer until I start to get tired, saying "Dad, I think I need to get some rest. Call you later when Mom's home?"

"Sure," he answers.

And just as I'm about to hang up the phone, my dad says, "I love you, kid."

"I love you too, Dad."

Finally, all these years later, after I had decided that "Same here, kid" was his way of saying "I love you," that really wasn't the case at all. He was more astute than I realized. Dad knew he only needed to say the words when I *really* needed to hear them. Sometimes parents do know better. . . . Turns out you don't need to hear "I love you" all the time to know you're loved.

Today, I see so many things that I've learned from my parents. As the proverb goes, "The apple doesn't fall far from the tree"—but since I'm Italian, it's probably more appropriate to say, "The fig doesn't fall far from the tree." I cook to feed the soul and the stomach. And yes, I have an extra lasagna in the freezer at this very moment in case you stop by. It's my way of saying "I love you."

Linda Kruse is a news correspondent, international spokesperson, corporate trainer, and documentarian. As a multi-award winning director, Linda's last documentary *KRUSING AMERICA* won sixty awards, earning her both

Filmmaker of the Year and Director of the Year. A best-selling author and an accomplished writer, she is currently featured in the #1 best-seller *Women Who Rock*. Also the owner of Atticus Productions, Inc., Linda has written, produced, and directed projects worldwide that explore challenging and intriguing topics while definitively capturing real people and the worlds they live in. All of Linda's work is presented with a creative elegance that is her signature style.

www.LindaKruse.com

How the Persistence of a Five-Year-Old Saved the Lives of Two Unborn Boys

Alex Lanshe

I never could have guessed that the lives of two unborn boys were in my hands that day, years before they were born. Had I known this, I certainly would have been more nervous. Why am I telling you this? Because my true and personal story contains a tremendous lesson that will give you a whole new perspective and appreciation for your life and daily struggle. In order to tell this story properly, I must travel back to when I was a little child.

When I was five years old, my parents enrolled me in martial arts classes. I remember in one particular class being asked to do an axe kick. After two failed attempts, I looked at the instructor and told him I couldn't do it. He said, "Try it again." I repeated that I could not. Then, very calmly but forcefully, the instructor said, "Then your class is over. Go sit outside and wait for the class to finish."

I remember walking off the mat, shocked and embarrassed. "How dare he make me sit out of class?" I said to myself. I proceeded to cry on the steps of the hallway for about twenty minutes. I cannot remember if my parents were attending and saw what happened or not. But I do remember my dad telling me later on in life, "I thought that was the end of martial arts for you. And since we were not particularly attached to it, we would have pulled you out if you didn't want to do it anymore."

The problem is that, had I quit that day, two little boys who were many years from being born could have died. I was obviously oblivious to this at the time, and many more events needed to transpire before I reached the life-saving moment, but this was one link in the chain. Let's finish connecting the links now.

Despite my embarrassing removal from class, I continued my training. I continued for the next twenty-one years, and I am still at it to this day. Now I am a national speaker and trainer for events ranging in size from large corporate keynote addresses to small businesses, entrepreneur groups, churches, high schools, universities, and private civilian groups concerned with their own right to self-defense. I am the author or co-author of three books; the founder of two websites, www.AlexLanshe.com and www.AnatomyOfaWarrior.com; and a reality-based personal protection trainer for private citizens as well as businesses, corporations, or private groups. I'm also a serial interviewer and blogger on the virtues and tactics of a warrior—and I accomplished this all before the age of thirty. I say all this not to impress you, but to impress upon you that NONE of this would have been possible had I quit martial arts at age five. Most importantly, I wouldn't have potentially saved the lives of two boys.

After my embarrassing removal from the mat at age five, I stayed at that same Dojo for one more year, and then my parents decided to move. They found another school in our new area, and I am still training with those instructors to this day, twenty-one years later. Without these instructors I would have never gone on to become a trainer and teacher myself. If I had not become an instructor, I never would have been able to save the lives of two children because I never would have been able to train their mother. I met this young woman at a party when I was nineteen and she was sixteen. She was quite pretty, and we shared a lot of things in common. We quickly became friends and have been for many years. A few years after we met, she expressed interest in doing some martial training. In one of our private classes, I taught her how to fall in such a way as to prevent injury. (In a fight, you may lose your balance or be forced down by the attacker, so learning how to fall properly is a critical skill.)

After teaching her for a few classes, we stopped the lessons because she was busy with other interests. Fast forward two to three years later when my friend was married and pregnant with her first child. When she was eight months pregnant, she tripped going up the stairs with her baby-bump pointing directly at the edge of a step. Instead of falling on the bump and potentially injuring or killing the baby, she did her front break fall and saved the child. This happened again around eight months with her second child.

Do I know those unborn boys would have died had I not taught her how to fall? No. However, I do know that if she lacked that skill, she may have fallen on them and injured them or they could have died. What I do know for certain is that because she knew how to fall and protect herself and her babies from harm, she doesn't have to visit two little tombstones each year. She has the freedom to speculate "what might have happened" because she fell properly and saved her children.

How does this story apply to you? Because had I quit all those years ago at age five, two little boys may have died. I had no way of knowing this at the time, but this is why persistence is so important—your vision is so limited, so small, that you most likely cannot see who will be affected if you quit. What is the thing you do that others are counting on you to do? Maybe it's being a good mom or dad; maybe it's running your business the right way so can support your family and employees. No matter what it is for you, do not quit. Bear the suffering with patience because you just might save someone's life later that you are only able to save because you persisted and didn't give up. Keep going—more people's lives are at stake than just yours; maybe even the lives of people who have yet to be born. Persist and fight on!

Alexander Lanshe was born in Akron, Ohio, and is the oldest of seven children. He is a national speaker (for large or small groups), author of three books, founder of www.AlexLanshe.com, blogger, serial interviewer, and reality-based personal protection trainer to civilians and former military and professional protectors from across the nation.

Alexander has trained with former and current members of the US Marines, US Secret Service, US Army Rangers, Navy SEALS, and has interviewed over 100 of the top protectors in the country, including Lt. Col. Dave Grossman, Gavin de Becker, and Massad Ayoob.

www.AlexLanshe.com

FLYIN' HIGH

Janie Lidey

One of the most vivid dreams I have during my sleeping hours is one I have dreamt over and over again. I started having this dream when I was a little girl, and when I am in it, I know that my only requirement for succeeding is that I must believe with all of my might that I can fly. I am simply standing on the ground and with complete faith and one giant leap, I begin to soar. There is no fear in my dream (in fact I know that if I allow even the slightest amount of fear to creep in, I will not be successful), and I know that all I must truly do is act as if I can fly, and I do. My flying dream has taught me that I can do anything I imagine. As long as I calm my fear, act as if, and leap with faith, I end up flyin' high!

As far back as I remember having my flying dreams, I also remember having daydreams about spreading peace and love across our planet. I know, it sounds kinda corny, but at twelve years of age, I had a sense that this was my purpose on earth. I became a singer-songwriter in the sixth grade, and when I began to play my songs for people, I realized that music would be my vehicle for creating the change I wanted to see in the world. The music I wrote seemed to lift people up, encourage kindness, and bring a sense of calm and even healing to them. I remember thinking, *What if my music could help spread that peace and love across the land?*

While songwriting was my deepest passion and created an amazing path for me, I was also being called to become a teacher. When I went to college, I majored in music education. Upon graduation I was given the most incredible opportunity, not only to teach our youth, but also to live a life that would fuel the writing I would continue to do through the years. My first job offer was in Seattle, but I decided to accept an offer that required me to calm my fear, act as if, and leap with faith. The job was in a remote, fly-in-only village called Kwigillingok, Alaska!

Two roads diverged in a wood and I—I took the one less traveled by,
and that has made all the difference.
Robert Frost

The road to Alaska was my road less traveled. Just a few weeks after my December graduation, I boarded a plane in sunny San Francisco, flew to Seattle, changed planes, and headed for Anchorage. There I boarded a smaller plane from Anchorage to Bethel, where I changed planes again and boarded a little Cessna that took me out to the village of Kwigillingok (a.k.a. Kwig) Alaska. I hopped off the Cessna onto a dogsled pulled by a snow machine and was whisked off to my village housing on the banks of the Kuskokwim River. The temperature was nearly 100 degrees colder in Kwig than it was just hours earlier when I left San Francisco! There were only a few hours of daylight at that time of year in Alaska, and what might have been a cozy drive to school in a heated car had I taken the job in Seattle was instead a ride in the dark from one end of the village to the other on my snow machine in 20 degrees below zero. There was no running water in Kwig, so my bathroom consisted of a honey bucket for a toilet and a cold, wet cloth for bathing each day. My adventures in Kwig were the beginning of a journey that would shape me into the writer and leader I would become.

After traveling as an itinerant music teacher in the villages for three years, I moved to Anchorage, where I spent the remainder of my teaching career. And while I was excited about the positive change I was making in my school setting, that big dream I had as a kid kept coming back to me. That childhood dream of spreading peace and love across the planet made me want to shift out of teaching in one building and make the whole world my classroom. I decided to calm my fear, act as if, leap with faith, and take an early retirement from teaching. I immersed myself in writing so I could get back to the dream of using my music to create the positive change I wanted to see in the world.

Seventeen years of teaching in the most diverse high school in the nation taught me so much about what really matters in life. The lessons I learned are the lessons I share on the stages I now speak and sing from. Love without condition. Leap with faith. Live in gratitude. Laugh while you're crying. Dream big. Use your imagination. Lead with love. I know that my recent success has come from applying these principles in every present moment. I believe it is why I was invited to co-write songs in Nashville with John Carter Cash and friends and sing at Willie Nelson's eightieth birthday tribute. I believe it is why I have platinum album musicians playing on my albums. I believe it is why I am being invited to share my message on stages all over the country. I believe it is why people are sharing their stories with me about how my music and message is lifting them up and changing their lives. I believe it is why I was presented with the Rock Star Inspiration Award for 2016.

I know that we all have a gift to share with the world. My gift shines brightest when I share my message through my music. It is my deepest desire to inspire you to lean into your gift and use it to create positive change on our beautiful planet. And just remember, as long as you calm your fear, act as if, and leap with faith, you'll end up flyin' high!

———————————

Janie Lidey is a professional speaker, Emmy Award-winning songwriter, Grammy Award-winning music educator, and Amazon #1 best-selling author. Janie speaks and sings at events across the country, encouraging her audiences to lean into their gift, calm their fear, and leap with faith into their life of purpose. She and her husband, Sean, currently live with their son, Tristan, in the log home they built on a hillside in Alaska fifteen years ago. They share their yard with the occasional moose, black bear, brown bear, and lynx, but their favorite four-legged friend is their yellow lab, Beaver.

www.JanieLidey.com

SETTNG GOALS DOESN'T WORK!

Steve Love

What? Writing down goals is probably the most fundamental part of any success course in existence, so how can I say they don't work?

This may be a very controversial chapter—Craig may even kick me out of his book!

But I still say that goal setting doesn't work. At least not most of the time. Neither does visualizing, affirmations, positive thinking, vision boards, self-help books and tapes and CDs, success seminars, or even fire walking. Yes, I've done them all; I've even jumped off the top of a telephone pole and bungee jumped off a bridge.

Let me make one big confession: I'm a personal development nut and have been one my whole adult life. I've read all the books, listened to all the tapes and CDs and have attended numerous weekend or longer success seminars from the best out there like Jim Rohn, Tony Robbins, Jack Canfield, Mark Victor Hansen, Harv Eker, Brian Tracy, and on and on. I even spent a day privately with Earl Nightingale once.

I enjoyed them all, and I'm sure I benefitted to some extent.

So back to goals. In any list of goals I've ever written and any other list I've seen from other folks, probably 70 to 90 percent or more are never fulfilled. If goals work so well, then why do they fail some 80 percent of the time? And when individuals don't achieve their goals, they often feel like a failure, so their self-esteem can be really damaged.

Looking back, my major achievements in life, such as graduating from college, marrying the girl of my dreams, having kids, running a successful real estate investment group, and becoming a speaker on cruise ships all over the world were never on any of my goal lists in the first place.

So what gives? I met a friend named Jack who opened my eyes.

He taught me that most of the goals on my lists were not really "core desires." All my major achievements were these core desires. On a scale of 1 to

100, these core desires are a 100, not even a 99. With a core desire, one becomes unstoppable.

Water won't boil at 211 degrees. It takes 212 degrees. Likewise core desires are all 100 on the scale. If a desire is only a 50, perhaps you'll get halfway there. Until it's 100, you can't be sure you'll ever achieve it.

Furthermore, those core desires stir up inside us something called the conquering force. This conquering force acts upon your core desire until it's achieved. You're unstoppable!

So how can you determine if your goal is a real core desire or not? Just ask yourself two questions:

What would I love to have, be, or do that I don't have now? (Don't consider money, time or any other limitations.)

If I had that or was that or did that, how would it make me *feel*?

Ask question number two for each entry on your list from question number one. This second question may be asked more than once—even several times—to help you dig down deeper to reach your real core desires. This should help you eliminate minor frivolous desires. Often true core desires will draw a very emotional response such as great joy, excitement, passion, or even tears.

Hawaii? Nah, I don't like beaches and I've been there many times.

New car? I already have four cars.

A new suit? No, I don't even like getting dressed up.

A family cruise to Alaska? Now we're talking! I'm excited. I can't wait!

Once you have your shorter list of what you think are your core desires, you must determine the intensity of your desires, feelings, and emotions on the 1 to 100 scale.

Only core desires are 100 on the scale, not even a 90 or a 95. These are not mere wants or wishes. These are the source of unbridled enthusiasm, discipline, and even excitement. They are what will enable you to overcome any roadblocks and provide you with undying persistence and discipline.

It's the core desires that then bring forth that conquering force from deep within you. When you tap into it, you'll feel excited, alive, happy, and passionate. You'll just "know" that you'll be achieving your core desires. You'll be relentless. It's almost as good as done!

Another friend and mentor, Bob, recently told me that goals are really an outdated technology. I must agree.

Yes, it will take some practice on your part to get to your real core desires, but it will get easier and easier.

Besides running a business that I love that allows me to help others and give back (two of my core desires) and living with the girl of my dreams (another core desire), I've recently visited the Great Wall of China, cruised around Japan, drove to and fished in Mexico, started another new business (all core desires), and on and on.

So, at the risk of offending just about every personal development guru out there, just forget about goals. Instead, learn how to identify your true core desires and tap into your conquering force within.

Then you will achieve everything you *really* want and live a truly fulfilled and happy life.

————————————

Steve Love is a successful real estate investor, broker, trainer, and blogger. He is the co-executive director, along with his wife Robyn, of Prosperity Through Real Estate, an educational real estate investors association (REIA) in Los Angeles and Las Vegas. He speaks on cruise ships throughout the world and is the author or co-author of several real estate and success books.

www.ProsperityThroughRealEstate.com

ROCK YOUR SELF-CONFIDENCE

Miss Winnie

G rowing up as a shy, introverted kid, I found myself spending lots of time alone. My asthma didn't help much. It was so bad that many nights I would sleep sitting up just so I could breathe. Having such a hard time breathing limited me in actively participating in lots of outside activities. Yet, although I kept to myself, attention always seemed to find me.

"Beauty isn't about having a pretty face. It is about having a pretty mind, a pretty heart, and most importantly, a beautiful soul." —Author Unknown

All while growing up, people always complimented me on my eyes. For me, that was unwanted attention. I was a kid and just wanted to be left alone. I just wanted to find some fresh air, so I could breathe and not feel like I was tired 24/7.

When I was in the fourth grade, my mother received a letter from the school district stating that I was gifted. At first, she didn't understand what the letter meant and got quite upset. The letter said I was a straight "A" student and should attend a certain school for "gifted" children—more unwanted attention drawn to me. From the fourth grade until junior high, I was bussed to various schools to attend the "gifted" program. Little did I know, all during this time, my sister was secretly vying for her own attention and growing jealous of the unwanted attention I was receiving.

"Jealousy is just a lack of self-confidence." —Author Unknown

Over the years I began to notice that every time I had any interaction with my dad, my sibling would find a way to interfere, demean, or put me down. She would even go the extra mile to "one up" me on anything and everything I did or said, to garner her own attention. She became extremely skilled at manipulating my father into believing she was an angel while stonewalling me to bring me down—all for the sake of attention.

"Avoid negative people at all costs.
They are the greatest destroyers of self-confidence and self-esteem."
—Brian Tracy

Two weeks before a well-deserved three-day holiday weekend, my sibling decided she wanted to throw my dad an eightieth birthday party. The expectation (for her) was for everyone to drop what they were doing and attend the event. It was time for me to put my foot down and teach others to respect my personal boundaries; it was time for me to learn to say no. That event was nothing more than another grandiose opportunity to humiliate and demean me in front of my entire family, friends, and guests. I declined the invitation.

"It's not selfish to LOVE yourself, take care of yourself,
and to make your happiness a priority. It's necessary."
—Mandy Hale

Professionally I seemed to attract the same type of people. They were called micromanagers. They were those managers who discouraged others from making decisions. They de-motivated their team and disempowered their staff. I became a victim of circumstance.

"Don't ever let anyone dull your sparkle."
"If you want to fly, give up everything that weighs you down."
—Authors Unknown

For about five years, I attended public speaking classes to help me find my voice. Public speaking helped build my self-confidence. It helped me speak a bit more confidently. It has been said, public speaking is the number one fear next to death—I was dying a slow death. As the walls of my world slowly crumbled around me, the pressures became too exhausting. The final straw came when I was called a "pushover" by one of my close male friends. That was it! It was time I spoke up! It was time I stop letting others run over me like a doormat.

I finally did what I do best—I started writing. As I wrote about my life's experiences, I began to see the patterns. "The writing was on the wall," and it truly helped me to clearly see the big picture of how others were writing *my* life's story. That was the defining moment, the beginning of the end. It was at that time that I fully claimed my self-confidence.

"Your journey has molded you for your greater good, and it was exactly what
it needed to be. Don't think that you've lost time.
It took each and every situation you have encountered to
bring you to the now. And now is right on time."
—Asma Tyson

While on a path for healthier living, my phenomenal primary care physician gently pushed me into a healthier lifestyle and motivated me to make long-term healthy life changes. My motivating personal trainer passionately pushed me beyond my limits and helped shape my mind, body, and spirit. My close friends—well, they are the best. They've helped to keep me grounded and have given me undivided support.

However, the number one person I continuously give thanks and honor to is God. He has always been by my side. He has guided me, supported me, picked me up when I have fallen, and provided me with the resources and lessons I needed to be successful during my life's journey. He gave me the strength to keep pushing on when no one else believed in me.

When I finally built up my self-confidence, I knew I had just learned to love myself—all of me—inside and out. I no longer feared speaking up! I no longer allowed others to walk all over me. Today I speak boldly with intellect. I no longer hush my voice for someone's comfort, and I speak my mind, even if it makes people uncomfortable.

*"Loving ourselves through the process of owning our story
is the bravest thing we will ever do."*
—Brene Brown

"Self-confidence affects all facets of one's life. Love yourself more than anything else in this world. Everything else, will take its rightful place. Claim it. Own it, then rock it!"
—Miss Winnie

Miss Winnie is a professional speaker and a #1 best-selling author. She is a graduate of the University of Southern California (USC) with an emphasis in communication. For over ten years she has been teaching women how to communicate better behind closed doors. She is passionate about helping women build their self-confidence so they can claim it, own it, then rock it!

www.RockYourSelfConfidence.com

I read inspirational books about grief, single motherhood, and creating a life with a "new normal." I talked to other single moms. I was uplifted by other people's experiences.

My girlfriends and Sean's teachers, from kindergarten through high school, were the other members of the "village" who helped raise him. Both he and I could go to them for objective perspectives when we locked horns, Irish against Irish.

Fast-forward twenty-four years: In 2013 my dream of opening my own business came true.

In May 2017, with his proud mama in the stands and his dad and grandmother looking on, Sean graduated from California State University at Fullerton with a degree in business. He is SO much like his dad: exactly the same kind of hair, intuitive, laid-back, nonjudgmental, humorous, athletic. And stubborn. We love hanging out together.

We did it, Sean and I, one foot in front of the other.

Debbie McCormick is a LinkedIn expert, speaker, author of the Amazon #1 best-seller *The LinkedIn Manual for Rookie*s, and contributing author to the *Women Who Rock* anthology. Her online courses teach business people how to increase their bottom lines through easily attracting, connecting to, and doing business with their ideal clients through LinkedIn.

www.DebbieMcCormick.com

DISCOVER YOUR THINNER SELF

David Medansky

I t's the smallest changes done consistently over a period of time that can make the biggest difference to successfully lose weight and keep it off.

Are you overweight? Do you need or want to lose ten, twenty, thirty, fifty pounds, or more, but you can't get on NBC's smash reality TV show, *The Biggest Loser*? Have you lost weight only to gain it back? Are you tired of being on the weight loss roller coaster? You are not alone. Today, over 70 percent of the US adult population is either overweight or obese. In 2013, 108 million people in the US were on diets. Of those, 90 percent were women. An estimated 45 million Americans go on a diet each year.

Most people who need to lose weight, but not extreme weight, find it difficult to get help. Let's be honest. Weight loss and exercise programs are expensive, time-consuming, or require more discipline than most individuals, including myself, have. Generally, those who want to shed weight are not motivated enough or committed enough to do something about it.

I've been where you are. I know what it's like. So who am I and why should you listen to me? My name is David Medansky. I wasn't always fat. Truth is, most of my life, I was fit and trim. But, as with many of us, life got in the way. I got lazy and self-indulgent. I stopped exercising regularly and started eating more junk food. Without realizing it, the weight crept up on me.

If you look at me now, you'd never suspect I was ever fat. I was uncomfortable. I was embarrassed and disappointed in myself. I tried and tried, but I couldn't stop eating or stay on a diet. Instead of eating one scoop of ice cream, I'd eat an entire pint in one sitting. I was disgusted with myself. I couldn't believe how my pants size ballooned up. But then something clicked inside me.

In July 2016, my doctor told me I had a 95 percent chance for risk of a heart attack. He said I had a choice. Either lose weight or find a new doctor, because he didn't want me dying on his shift. At that moment I made the decision to shed the unwanted and unhealthy pounds. That began my weight loss journey. Over the next four months, I lost more than fifty pounds; over 25 percent of my total weight. Now I feel great and have more energy. I don't need to take a nap in the afternoon. So I believe it's my duty and obligation to assist others lose weight they need to or want to, so they don't suffer like I used to.

People who are overweight are at risk for developing serious health problems, such as heart disease, diabetes, high blood pressure, high cholesterol, stroke, arthritis, and gallbladder disease, just to mention some of the risks. These health issues can be prevented. People can live healthy lives simply by changing their eating habits and lifestyle. My new mission and life's purpose is to help others shed their unwanted pounds and keep them off. It was so scary for me, I don't want anybody else to have to go through the pain, discomfort, and worry of being overweight or obese.

Being an author, I decided to write about my weight loss journey and incredible transformation to support others achieve their weight loss goals. Losing weight is one of the most difficult things to do. No one is telling you it will be easy. It's not. But if I can do it, and others have done it, you can do it too!

Nobody undertakes a weight loss program to fail. Yet many do fail because their weight loss is only a temporary fix. If you're going to have permanent success shedding those unwanted pounds, you'll need to make lifestyle changes.

In doing research for my forthcoming book, *Discover Your Thinner Self,* I was overwhelmed and inundated with the amount of information available for weight loss. I learned that there are many misconceptions and false beliefs about weight loss and dieting. A misconception is a view or opinion that is incorrect because it is based on false evidence, faulty thinking, or understanding. There are several trains of thought about losing weight that are not true or only partially true. Unfortunately too many people trying to lose weight are vulnerable to misinformed individuals or those simply wanting to rip them off.

So how do you protect yourself? It is always good to question weight loss statements presented as fact. Too often there are many perceived facts perpetuated by certain groups and businesses about dieting and weight loss that are untruthful, fabricated, or inaccurate. Believing some of these may actually inhibit you from achieving your true, long-term weight loss goal.

You can get a free report titled *Common Misconceptions About Diet and Weight Loss and Questions You Should Ask Before Enrolling in Any Weight Loss Program* simply by going to www.DiscoverYourThinnerSelf.com and requesting a copy.

There is no secret to losing weight. If someone tells you they have a secret method to dropping weight, it's a gimmick. There is no amount of money you can pay to get the desired results you want without putting in the time, effort, and doing the work. Nobody can do for you what you must do for yourself to get rid of unhealthy weight. No other person can exercise for you. No one can eat healthier for you. No one can drink the necessary amount of water for you. Only you can take control of your weight loss issue.

Making the decision to reduce weight and get slimmer can change your life for the better and improve your overall health. But without following through and persevering during difficult periods, you'll most likely fail. John D. Rockefeller said, "Perseverance . . . overcomes almost everything." If you take action and are tenacious in your efforts, you will succeed.

Mark Twain said, "Twenty years from now you will be more disappointed by the things that you didn't do than by the ones you did do." Isn't it time you started your weight loss journey today?

David Medansky, born and raised in the Chicago metropolitan area, graduated from the University of Arizona School of Law in 1991. He's a best-selling author, attorney, and trusted weight loss advisor and consultant. His forthcoming weight loss book, *Discover Your Thinner Self*, will be available soon.

www.BeyondLosingWeight.com

Recovering and Rocking Your Life at Any Age

Crystal Meisner

As I was growing up, all I ever heard folks talk about was getting married, having children, working twenty-five to forty years at a profession, and retiring with a gold watch. Having retirement savings to pay for your "sunset years." Paying off your house and car, reducing your monthly expenses. Then dying and leaving it all to your kids so "they wouldn't have it as hard as you did."

What a pipe dream! As I grew older and matured in my world involvement, everything I'd been led to believe was turning out to be a grand fallacy. So how was I to achieve an ideal life, financial stability, and enjoy my golden years? Is it possible? It's become the question we must all answer, and the answers are as individual as we are.

I had passed the half-century mark, and my life was NOTHING that I had grown up believing it should be, despite working in a field I enjoyed. No, it had gone down a dramatically different path, one I could never have envisioned. I struggled, working hard to achieve everything I ever had in order to create some semblance of an acceptable lifestyle for my Down Syndrome son and myself. I gave my all to everything I did, until I was diminishing into a ghost of myself. I had a health condition that literally drained me of my life force, sucking me into a world of lethargy and hopelessness. I was half-dead and barely functioning. But still, I got up, and got it done, as best I could.

Then I got a warning. On Christmas Eve morning 2012, I collapsed upon exiting the shower. We were vacationing in the Tonto National Forest, and my healthcare plan at the time wouldn't pay for service there, so I didn't seek medical help. I suspected the cause, what would be needed, and was not going to attempt that treatment out of state. I spent the rest of the vacation in bed, trying to regain my strength so I could drive home at the end of our stay. But I knew I was facing a much-needed surgery, or I could die.

After I changed my health insurance plan, I had the procedure to correct the condition. Within the short recovery period, I started feeling so much better that I determined I did not want to grow old, decrepit, and sit around complaining about my aches and pains, like so many seniors I'd encountered.

I went on a mission.

First, to recover my health—to shed the weight I gained over the last thirty years, to improve my fitness and flexibility, to find a more sustainable healthiness. I started a nutrition program that provided custom dietary menus I could not only follow, but enjoy and stick with, and I started increasing my activity level. I got back to participating in my life instead of watching it slip by. And then, in September 2014 I went to a self-improvement seminar on creating a sustainable financial future.

I had opened myself up to change and improvement. I was ready for it and actively seeking it. And the universe obliged.

At that seminar, I had a lightning-bolt-to-the-brain epiphany. Utilizing all the teachings and life lessons I had garnered, I was given a concept to create a program to help others. Mind-boggling! I had two sets of notes going—one for what was being taught from the stage, and one for the data that was downloading in my brain.

Wait. What? Who, ME? I had spent twenty-eight years working mostly for various government and cable entities, producing local television shows, and operating cablecast TV stations. What did I know about entrepreneurship, creating and operating my own coaching business, holding seminars, etc.? I needed to learn!

Fortunately, I love to learn. I'm extremely curious about how things and people work, and at that event, I found some other entrepreneurs who offered programs I felt could aid me. Craig Duswalt was one of them. And as they say, the rest is history. Well, to be accurate, it was the beginning of HER STORY— my new one. I embarked upon a new journey, met new people, and encountered new concepts, ideas, and methods. I was constantly learning, evaluating, devising, refining, and working on putting together this initial epiphany project. But before I was finished, there was more to come.

The universe knew its plan, and the epiphany was only the impetus to put me where God wanted me. Because the universe knew I had more to offer and more gifts to give. There were people whose lives I needed to impact, even BEFORE that program was implemented. I hadn't spent all that time working in the TV industry to simply abandon that knowledge. The universe hadn't given me a child with special needs to ignore others' plights. And God hadn't made me a repository of knowledge for it to die with me. So I was given other epiphanies, other tasks to accomplish, other projects to do, other programs to build, other people to help. The universe provided me with more resources, more tools, and the courage and impetus to move forward. There is much I have currently in progress, and it will come as the universe decrees. I do believe God has shown me the path He wants me to take. There really is no other way to describe all the changes that have occurred in three short years. Those who knew me before are astounded at the changes they've seen. It'll be a lot of work, but I'm excited to tackle it.

Recently, I took a big step, a massive leap of faith, holding on to the vision I've been given, and I *retired* from that government job to dedicate myself full-time to building these projects and my new life. And I realized a couple of things. There had been many times in my younger years when I'd actually *been* an entrepreneur! OK, I can *do* this! Additionally, I've come to realize that a "midlife crisis" is an awareness that one has not fulfilled his or her purpose in life. Too many try to change their surroundings instead of themselves. One should change only what is necessary to support and encourage the discovery and giving of the gift each one of us has, not to ruin others' lives as we seek to find our own. Your closest family and friends may only need *your* change to inspire change in themselves. So do yourself and the world a favor—regardless of your age, Go Rock Your Life!

Crystal Meisner's thirty years' work in local television and cable has been seen on PEG, PBS, MTV, ESPN, HGTV, and more. For four decades, she has been on stage, screen, and behind the scenes for a wide variety of productions and shows and has been privileged to work with many notables in entertainment, government, and history. She was an AMPAS Student Awards Finalist, an International CINDY Awards Judge, and made an appearance on *Oprah*. Under her guiding tenet of service, she has coached Special Olympians, and helps wherever, whenever, and whomever she can.

www.meiamtv.com

JOURNEY TO MY DREAMS

Debbie Morgan

When I was in high school, attending college was never a consideration. No one in my family attended, and it was expensive. It was business school for me.

I loved learning about accounting and taxes and eagerly looked forward to getting my first job and earning a living. While I was business school, my family was blindsided by news that my sister was in a near-fatal accident. Over the next six weeks, the ICU waiting room became my study hall. Amazingly, my sister made a full recovery—and I graduated number one in my class.

Landing what seemed to be an ideal job in the construction loan department of a bank, I soon became bored. I realized I needed variety and wanted something more. I wondered what profession would allow me to work with numbers, help people, and feed my love of learning. I decided working for a CPA firm would be perfect. I soon obtained a job as a junior bookkeeper. I was really happy learning from the CPAs there and taking college classes in the evening.

After starting with the CPA firm, my husband became a firefighter with odd hours and days away at the station. So it wasn't a problem when we both learned of the new term *tax season* and the hours that came along with it. Life moved along nicely, and we were blessed with two amazing sons. I am forever grateful for family members who stepped up and made it possible for us to pursue our careers during those times.

I never had the lofty goal of being a CPA, but after ten years of working for the firm, one of the partners asked me about taking the CPA exam. I was stunned.

Soon after, I discovered that I could take the exam without having a degree. I had the required accounting experience, the required number of college units (after all, I was in my tenth year of night school!), and the partners who could verify my experience.

At the time, the exam had four parts: Audit, Law, Tax, and Practice and

Theory. I studied like a maniac. Between working full-time, a hubby with a funky schedule, and two very active boys, I was greatly challenged. I spent all my spare time attending review courses and taking practice tests.

Finally the time came to take the exam. When I got to the testing site, everyone looked terrified. I felt better knowing I wasn't alone. But I was sadly mistaken thinking that I could pass the exam because of my work experience. The exam was brutal! I waited for my results and when they came, I had only passed one part—Practice and Theory. I was devastated. Maybe my inner voice was right: "I can't be a CPA. What was I thinking?"

Though my confidence was destroyed and I considered not taking the exam again, I felt like so many people were depending on me. After much deliberation, I decided to change my study approach. Passing only two parts was required to continue on in the testing process. So rather than study for four parts equally, I selected Practice and Theory, as well as Audit. However, my husband convinced me to sign up for all four parts even if I didn't study all of the parts. I reluctantly agreed.

Taking the exam was just as scary the second time around.

After waiting what seemed to be forever, the results came. I couldn't believe it! I passed two parts all right: Practice and Theory again and . . . what? Tax? That's not the second part I had studied! If I had not listened to my husband, I would have only passed one part and would have had to start the process all over again.

Over the next year, I passed the exam and had the partners sign off on the experience section as I eagerly waited to be certified. All was good . . . until it wasn't. I received a letter from the State Board of Accountancy indicating they wanted to review my experience. I could go to Los Angeles, but if I wanted to expedite the process, I would have to go to San Francisco.

I was tired of waiting to be a CPA and just wanted to be done, so off to San Francisco I went. The review was held in the dank basement of the hotel. The other candidates all had files in their hands; I was the only one who brought boxes. We were all terrified. When my name was called, I was led into a large conference room, where I sat frozen in fear and somehow answered the questions thrown at me.

Needing to chat among themselves, I was asked to leave. Struck by terror, I felt like my life was in their hands. I waited for what seemed like forever before they called me back. They gave me their results, and I began to cry. With confusion on their faces, they asked what was wrong. I explained I was so disappointed. They chuckled and said that I *did* pass. Oh boy, even with two hearing aids, my fear distorted what I heard!

Being a CPA was amazing, but there was one more thing I still had to do. After eighteen years of night classes, I finally earned my bachelor's degree in accountancy. That felt good.

Two years after becoming a CPA, I became partner of the firm where it all began. But I wasn't satisfied. I didn't feel like we were making a difference or working with the type of clients I wanted to help—small businesses and non-profits. But I couldn't do anything about it—I didn't have the confidence to leave and start my own practice. I dreaded the thought of starting over, and I worried about how I would do it financially.

Then something happened that changed everything: The partners didn't get paid for six weeks. This was disturbing. Then, a lightbulb went on. If working there meant being unhappy and not getting paid, I might as well as start my own practice! This didn't seem so terrible after all.

Deborah Morgan and Company, Inc., opened its doors eleven years ago.

I never dreamed it was possible to be a CPA with my own corporation! I have employees I love, clients I love, and I feel like I'm really making a difference. There are days when I walk in my office and get goose bumps. I get to do what I want, when I want . . . I am so blessed.

Debbie Morgan, CPA, is the founder of Deborah Morgan and Company, Inc., a full-service tax and accounting firm that provides services to entrepreneurs, individuals, and nonprofits. Debbie's passion is helping business owners overcome their fears of dealing with their accounting and tax matters so they can focus on their passion—their own business.

She consults regularly with her clients to help them understand their finances and taxes, enabling them to reduce their tax liability and increase their bottom line. Her firm provides bookkeeping and payroll services as well as tax representation before the Internal Revenue Service and Franchise Tax Board.

www.DeborahMorganCPA.com

A LOVE STORY

David Nassaney

My wife Charlene and I had a fairy-tale courtship, romance, and marriage for the first twenty-one years of our lives together.

Then one morning, Charlene complained of a bad headache that she'd been having for a few days. We didn't pay much attention to it. But then, the headache ceased being only a headache.

By the time the ambulance arrived, it was too late.

The woman I loved had a massive stroke and became severely speech impaired and paralyzed on her right side. Our world immediately turned upside down, and our lives have never been the same.

Instead of entering the empty-nest phase of life that we always looked forward to, I found myself having to constantly care for the love of my life 24/7. There is no way that anyone can ever prepare for that.

To be honest, the first two years were a living hell for us. I didn't know what I was doing. I didn't know how to care for my wife. And I didn't know who Charlene was anymore.

Charlene became angry and bitter because she was no longer the woman that she was before; I became angry and bitter for the same reasons. I grieved that my wife was no longer the woman that I married. I still loved her, but it was very hard being on the receiving end of her anger brought about by her grief.

I felt so guilty. In fact, I came to a point that I didn't know if I could do it any longer.

One day, I sat down and wrote her a letter: "Charlene, you are so mean to me. It's so hard being your husband taking care of you all the time without feeling any love in return. I know it's hard for you, but you are making it even harder for me to care for you. I just don't know if I can be with you any longer. I'll take care of you financially, but I don't think I can be with you."

I read that letter over and over again, but I just couldn't give it to her. It is truly how I felt in that moment. But I wanted to love my wife. I wanted to care for her. I wanted to have a loving relationship with the woman that I had married so many years ago, but it seemed impossible. I really didn't know how to care for my wife anymore. I didn't know if I even wanted to. I wondered if there was any hope for us.

So rather than separate or divorce, I decided I just had to get out of the house. I left her mother in charge, and I hopped on a plane to visit some friends and relatives out of state for the weekend. I just had to think and get some perspective.

When I returned, I felt extremely rested and recharged. It felt so good. I had a much better outlook and attitude. I even remembered that someone at the hospital invited me to a caregiver's support group for people just like me: burned-out caregivers. Going to that group changed everything for me. I found hope again, and I discovered that I had to take care of me before I could take care of my wife.

They tell us on airplanes that in the event of an emergency, we are to put our oxygen mask on first before we attempt to help our loved ones with their masks. That's such a great metaphor for all of life: You have to take care of yourself first, not out of selfishness, but out of survival. If I couldn't take care of me, how could I possibly take care of Charlene?

When I finally realized how much I was able to change, to my surprise, my wife also changed. I was no longer thinking about how she made me feel. I was just taking care of me, so I could take care of her.

After two years, Charlene finally reached the acceptance stage of her grief, and she became her old self again. I am very proud of her. She was, and still is, a cross between Martha Stewart and Wonder Woman. She makes us "normal" people look like whiners and complainers. She is my hero!

Because of my experience, I realized that there are so many other caregivers out there taking care of a loved one—a spouse, a child, a parent, a sibling, a friend—all who had a tragic, unexpected incident in their lives. They're going through this incredible pain, feeling lost and alone, and I want to help them triumph over that pain. I don't want them to give up like I almost gave up. I don't want their relationships to suffer any more.

That's why I became Dave, the Caregiver's Caregiver. Now I host a weekly radio show and a private membership site for caregivers. I provide a wide range of resources—blogs, articles, and podcasts; interviews of those who survived and thrived; uplifting videos; and weekly conference calls. I also offer personal coaching. And I absolutely love it.

Without daily support and accountability, caregivers can't survive. They will be caught in a self-destructive death spiral. However, through the faith, hope, and love that I provide, caregivers can thrive and triumph over the urge to give up, just like I did.

Every caregiver's life is a love story. Let me help make that love story one of hope and triumph too.

To learn more about how I can help you or a caregiver you know, go to www.CaregiversCaregiver.com. While you are there, please take our short quiz, "Are You a Candidate for Burnout?" and I will send you a digital copy of my first book, *One Arm, One Leg, 100 Words: Overcoming Unbelievable Hardships*, absolutely free.

My new book, *It's My Life, Too! Reclaim Your Caregiver Sanity by Learning When to Say "Yes" and When to Say "No,"* is perfect for caregivers who know they should be putting their needs first but just don't know how.

David Nassaney is a USC graduate, entrepreneur, gas station owner, author, speaker, life coach, and host of *Dave, The Caregiver's Caregiver Radio Program*, yet his most important role is Caregiver to his lovely wife, Charlene, for over twenty-one years.

The mission of his Radio Show is to help Caregivers overcome adversity, the grief process, and burnout—as well as just having a place to rest, relax, and recharge their batteries.

On his extensive website, www.CaregiversCaregiver.com, you will find his blog, Caregiver resources, inspirational quotes, video and audio podcasts, books, and products he created to encourage Caregivers in their difficult journey.

www.CaregiversCaregiver.com

COUNT ON YOURSELF

TK O'Geary

As a kid, when someone asked me what I wanted to be when I grew up, the answer "a successful consultant" never came to mind. Yet years later I now help organizations excel in the people side of process and delighting customers. Strong mentors and self-determination made me a success instead of a negative statistic and helped me persist when I felt out of sync with those around me.

As a toddler my parents keenly responded to my childhood curiosity and desire to learn. Their action was key, as studies show that an unchallenged mind can result in slipping into the unproductive side of society. "I can't" was not an acceptable phrase in our house. Any hint of "can't" was met with helpful, and often fun, discussions about how one might figure out how to solve the problem. Even at a very young age, I learned that almost anything was possible.

Questions such as "What does that word mean?" were met with one of Dad's famous phrases, "Well, what does the dictionary say?" We would look it up and talk about its uses. This taught me to go to a reliable source to get answers. Making assumptions was not an acceptable practice.

Our exchanges went beyond dilemmas and definitions; we also played games, lots of games. Dad always played his best, including one-on-ones with me, and we'd talk about strategy and risks and how to do better. Eventually I started winning some, which was quite satisfying because they were *real* wins.

My parents' approach resulted in me walking early, reading early, and talking early (though today, I bet some wish I talked less!), so they enrolled me in school early. While my brain embraced the challenges, and I began to fall in love with math for its rules and clarity of truth, emotionally I was out of sync with the rest of the class and reluctant to join in at times. Bolstered by my parents' and teachers' challenges, encouragement, and raising of the bar, I learned to count on myself, figure out how to finish tasks, and sometimes feel like I fit in.

In college I landed an intern position doing analysis at a consulting firm.

163

Biggest Failure, the Biggest Breakthrough

George Partsalidis

Have you ever felt so grateful in your life for what you have, for whom you have become, and for all the loved ones you have to share your live with?

That is the feeling that rushed through my body as I sat to write these pages. Tomorrow is July 1, and up here in the Great White North, we will celebrate Canada's 150th birthday. Like every year, my beautiful wife and I will be taking out two adorable daughters and our six-year-old attention-seeker son to a variety of activities: parades, concerts, shows, and of course the fireworks finale at night. And I will be celebrating thirty-five years since I moved to Toronto from a tiny Mediterranean country that is a few thousand years older than Canada.

Yes, days like tomorrow, but also countless other times throughout the year, I do feel grateful for my family that I love and adore; I do feel grateful for the life I now have the privilege to enjoy.

But life hasn't always been like this. The road to the top was an adventurous journey with many disappointments and failures.

I grew up in the land of Gods and Heroes, in a small city in Greece between Mount Olympus and the hills and the prairies where Aristotle mentored and shaped the mind and spirit of Alexander the Great. I was taught that if you work hard, you are kind and help others, and believe in God, success will follow.

In my early teenage years I had come across a book by Walter Jermaine, *The Magic Power of Your Mind*, which introduced me to the power of the subconscious mind and visualization techniques. I was in heaven! I felt that I discovered a getaway to another dimension. There wasn't even a library nearby and bookstores were hours away with mostly traditional education books. Oh, how I wish there was Internet back then!

The years passed, and I found myself in Canada starting my own business. While attending a Young Entrepreneurs event, I talked to an extraordinary speaker that emphasized the power of belief and mentioned the law of attraction. He assured me that all would work out; what I needed was to study success and the laws that govern it and I would attract wealth and success in to my life. He introduced me to his "bible," Napoleon Hill's *Think and Grow Rich*. I bought his new book, he signed it for me, and off I went to conquer the world.

I did read his book. I liked it so much it became the only Christmas present I gifted to friends and family that year. Of course everybody was disappointed and thought I was going crazy. The title of the book was *You Were Born Rich* by Bob Proctor.

And then my search for enlightenment started. From Silva Mind Control Method workshops to Tony Robbins UPW seminars. From Wayne Dyer's one-day lectures to full weeks of Nero Linguistic Programming Certification Workshops with NLP cofounder Richard Bandler. And there were dozens of other seminars, books, and audiobooks that could possibly help break thought limitations and perceptions that prevented me from unleashing my full potential.

It all seemed to be going well. The future looked bright—until suddenly the tables turned, and I found myself hitting rock bottom. I could not explain it! I felt like life and God had forgotten me. I worked hard. I always did my best. I was always optimistic, but nothing would go my way. I kept failing in different businesses I had started. And I could not seem to find any meaningful relationships.

If that wasn't enough, my family and almost all of my friends abandoned me. Even though later I realized it was probably the best thing that could have happened to me, at that time I felt like a failure and thought my life did not really matter.

I was neutralized by an invisible force . . .

A thought, disbelief, fear . . .

An "entity" I could not identify . . .

I lost my business . . .

I was months behind in rent, and I owed thousands to my suppliers and employees.

I had no money to even buy food. I will never forget the day that I walked in to a grocery store with only 50 cents to see how much bread I could buy and wondering how long that could last me . . .

There, in the darkest moment, where all else failed, there was nothing to do. No one to see. Nowhere to go. There was no fear. No blame.

It was then that I found PEACE. Everything became so clear and simple.

All the knowledge and training just clicked in place. I finally had all the time in the world to actually apply what I had learned. It was not easy. Determination and repetition helped break old habits and created new ones that helped build the future I always wanted.

As Tony Robbins says: "What you *know* doesn't mean shit. What do you *do* consistently?"

Yes! I started all over again. In my early thirties. I went back to school and took computer classes during the day and worked two jobs at night.

Within a year I paid all the money I owed to my suppliers and employees. A year later I started a new business—now in its twentieth year—that flourished and became one of the most trusted floor and window covering stores in the Greater Toronto Area. I met and married my wife, Maria, the most productive woman I know!

Yes, I am very grateful.

As I end, I would like to echo through you some powerful words from James Allen's *As a Man Thinketh*:

> Man is the master of thought, the moulder of character, and the maker and shaper of condition, environment, and destiny. As a being of Power, Intelligence, and Love and the lord of his own thoughts, man holds the key to every situation, and contains within himself that transforming and regenerative agency by which he may make himself what he wills.

———————

George lives happily with his family in Toronto, Canada. He is an entrepreneur, a realtor, a mortgage agent, and still owns the successful flooring and window coverings store, Kingsway Carpets & Blinds.

His goal is to teach his children by example, to love life, to conquer their fears and to CREATE their dreams.

He is involved in community events, helping and spreading his knowledge of business and life success, and as a hobby he is a passionate and dedicated Kung Fu student and teacher.

www.GeorgePartsalidis.com

You Never Know What's Around the Corner

Suzy Prudden

When I started this story, I was going to talk to you about becoming homeless eight months after being featured on *The Oprah Winfrey Show*. But I've told that story. It was a rough experience, as I was a celebrity in the fitness world, had written eleven books on fitness and body/mind technology, had my own TV show on NBC in New York, and so on. By the time I was in my late thirties, I was a household name. I was my own brand. It sounds very glamorous to say, "I'm going on a twenty-two-city tour." The reality is that you see a lot of airports, taxies, hotel rooms, TV studios, radio stations, and newspaper offices. It's a bit grueling, although I did love it. But by the age of forty, I was totally burned out.

In 1983, at the age of forty, I sold my fitness school and basically retired. I just didn't know it then. All I did know was I didn't want to teach fitness anymore. I had discovered the mind and began exploring the body/mind connection and then created a whole new body of work around that area of life— again, very successfully. My name led me into a lot of exciting situations and experiences. I met a lot of incredible people, spoke on numerous stages, and taught at spas across the country and in Europe. Again, I was the brand.

It's funny, when I moved to California in 1985, I said I didn't want to be Suzy Prudden anymore. Do you know hard it is not to be who you are? Everywhere I went people knew who I was. Everything I did had my name on it. Even when I ran a weight loss hypnosis center with four offices in the Los Angeles area with another name on the business, it was still all about Suzy Prudden. I did the TV interviews; I was the one interviewed by the *LA Times* and the *Wall Street Journal*—it was still Suzy Prudden. My name has led my businesses for over fifty years. I used to joke about it at conferences and call myself a Big Deal (which definitely polarized people), but I was. I was not a Rock Star, but I taught a lot of their children.

My sister, Joan Meijer, has been working with me since the mid-80s. We've written five books together—again, with my name on the cover—and she's helped me in the various businesses I've created over the years. In 2006 we took a workshop in Las Vegas and were told little books were the new norm. We had always written big books, published by big publishing houses. Now we were told to write a little book and publish it ourselves. So we did. I ran the business while she wrote the book: *Suzy Prudden's Itty Bitty Weight Loss Book.* She designed the cover, and we purchased the obligatory two thousand copies. I think we have 1,800 left in our garage. We certainly knew how to write books for the big houses, but we hadn't a clue what to do in the self-publishing world.

I'm going to digress for a moment. My sister is probably the smartest person I know. She's been a writer her whole life. But she hasn't sold many books. About six or seven years ago, while having lunch with a friend, her friend told her of another friend who was making four to five hundred dollars a month writing short erotica stories and selling them on the Internet. My sister thought, *I can do that.* And she did. She learned all she needed to know to put her stories up on the various digital platforms on the Internet and within a few months was making money. It wasn't a lot of money. And then she called me one day to tell me that she had made $20K with her short stories that year on the Internet. But she was finding them very boring to write and wanted to stop. (She stopped writing these stories four years ago, and they are still selling; she's still getting paid).

Back to my original story: Joan came to visit over the Christmas holidays in 2014. I had been running my Suzy Prudden International Coaching/Hypnosis business since 2008 and really didn't want to anymore. I had asked her to change the weight loss book cover and make it a bit shorter. She did. With great trepidation she showed me the new cover but held her finger over the top part of the title. The cover was right for the book as we had used a similar picture in successful ads we ran in the *LA Times* when we had our weight loss center. Then she removed her finger and my name wasn't there. It was no longer *Suzy Prudden's Itty Bitty Weight Loss Book;* it was *Your Amazing Itty Bitty Weight Loss Book.* My ego had a moment.

My name had been first on everything for over fifty years. And now it wasn't. For someone who has had that positioning for that long, it's an interesting moment, and after I got over it, I saw its brilliance. As I looked at the book, I realized it was a company, and I didn't have to write the books anymore. My sister knew how to do the back end; get the books up on Amazon and all the digitals, as well as edit. I am the consummate salesperson. In that moment we both knew we had a million-dollar company, and we were total equals in the business. Neither one of us could do what the other could do, and we were both crucial to the business.

Now, rather than everything being Suzy Prudden, everything is about our authors. Joan and I have at least eighty-five years of experience between us in our field. It truly felt as if God had given us a gift. It still does. We were in business four days later, signed our first author two weeks after that, had our first book published eight weeks after that, and we've never looked back. And now the company is not about Suzy Prudden. It's about the incredible authors who are attracted to Itty Bitty Publishing where we help people use their books to build their own high six-figure business. And although I'm still Suzy Prudden, I'm not *that* Suzy Prudden.

Internationally acclaimed speaker, author, and seminar leader, Suzy Prudden is known as the experts' expert. Having had multiple businesses, she has taken her expertise in writing books and speaking on stages and TV and radio to build a publishing empire. Her motto: "A book is a business builder, not a business card." Her authors have been known to quadruple their income in less than two years using their books to market their business. You've seen her on *Oprah*, *The Today Show*, and *Good Morning America*, and she has been featured in the *New York Times*, the *LA Times*, the *Washington Post*, *People* magazine, *Vogue*, and *Newsweek*.

www.IttyBittyPublishing.com

THIS BEING HUMAN

Bart Rademaker, MD

How can we help humanity if we don't understand what it is to be "human"? How can we change anything if we don't understand what to change?

Einstein said: "We cannot solve our problems with the same level of consciousness that created them."

What is it to you to be human? In a past relationship, it was with much disdain that I reacted to my partner's excuses for her personal failures as "just being human!" She would constantly flaunt these excuses in my face, expecting me to accept them without question, when I very well knew she could have easily succeeded. It was frustrating because her failures affected my own existence and passion to achieve. Unknowingly, it was "I" that allowed it to thwart my impact on the world! The truth is, she was right in a way she did not understand, and wrong to choose to be at the effect of the world around her, like so many others.

My hastened response and accusation that she was playing the victim card was met with the same disdain I gave her. Not only was I right to accuse her but wrong as well, and I did not know it. My own naiveté attributed my inability to help her understand what she was really doing to my ineffective communication. To this day, she maintains that I am a poor communicator. The truth is, I did not understand the neuro strategies or brain strategies that caused her to choose the very behavior she displayed. I did not understand her system of mental processing—either conscious or unconscious. I also did not understand mine, and I am grateful for this lesson.

We live in an intelligent universe—nothing happens by random. You are indeed the culmination of all your actions, decisions, emotions, experiences and learnings to this very moment. It's your fault you picked up this book, are reading its pages, and learning from the many talented contributors—for which I am glad.

Whatever it is that we do always makes sense—even when it is out of our own awareness! Over time we have acquired or developed strategies for our own behavior. This is well illustrated in the science of neurolinguistic programming (NLP for short) that teaches us about "human" behavior. It is important to remember what you already know, that you have taken on many a strategy of someone else or someone else's prescription for their own successful behavior. All behavior is intended to achieve a specific result.

Since much of what we do is outside of our awareness, it is helpful to know that our conscious mind will process up to two hundred bits of information per second, and the unconscious two million bits per second. When we behave in a way that creates an "internal values" conflict, the battle which mostly happens in our unconscious, we consciously beat ourselves up. Most of us do a great job of it despite its unpleasantness. Question: What happens to you if you treated others in the same way you beat yourself up? Would you be without friends, families, co-workers, or even put in jail for the severity of your behavior towards others?

We give ourselves very little credit for who we really are as humans. If we do have to boost our self-esteem or ego, we lie to ourselves in a way that it is obvious to others, giving them cause for their displeasure, judgement, or rejection. You have seen it in others, and you've done it yourself! My own answer is to give myself permission to be "human," with my faults, weaknesses, my greatness, and magnificence. I don't lie to myself and say "I'm perfectly imperfect." That statement makes no sense, and for that matter it absolves one from any blame or responsibility for choices and actions. We are all to blame, and until we accept this and the consequences of our behavior, we will not change and grow or take credit for our own greatness so that we may expand our humanness.

What makes sense is that somehow you and I developed these attributes—good, ugly, or indifferent! I don't justify, explain, excuse, deny, or even understand them; rather, I embrace them all. I can fine-tune, adjust, or redirect them. I bring into my awareness who I am, what I really want, and who I wish to become more of. This is our growth. It creates change, enhances our lives, and brings us closer to the happiness and fulfillment we truly desire. There is no greater gift to self than to become the person you were meant to be and to offer the same gifts to the world around you. I know what I want to do for this world; this life needs me, and it needs you!

I am passionate about creating change, enhancing life, and establishing peaceful awareness. My emotional currency is to see the success in others. I believe that we live in an intelligent universe and all we have to do is tap into our own authentic genius and live the life we desire. It is about understanding which neuro strategies we use to achieve the specific intended results, consciously or unconsciously, by someone else's prescription or by our own. I also believe that we all desire divine happiness, but for that to happen, we must resolve whatever makes us unhappy. We must discover what we did not know that we did not know that makes the difference.

I have a media platform: Dr. Rademaker's Prescription for Your Transformation, bringing to you the new voices, new solutions to help you discover what you did not know that you did not know. I offer authentic conversations with real people and their success strategies, to help you find the answer you seek or the one you want to share. Together we can all help each other to a higher level of consciousness. Making success easy leads to more success. Modeling others or having a coach is one of the best strategies to success, as exemplified by one of the best strategists of today, Tony Robbins.

You too can participate. E-mail me at dr@drrademaker.com and share your own genius with someone that needs you, and reach higher levels of consciousness!

––––––––––––––––

Bart Rademaker, MD, is a plastic, reconstructive, and regenerative surgeon who has done pioneering work with stem cell surgery using autologous (the patient's own) tissue. Host of the media platform *Dr. Rademaker's Prescription for Your Transformation*, he is the #1 best-selling author of *52 Week Success Plan*. Dr. Rademaker is an international speaker and strategic coach and a professional photographer. He is certified in engergy healing and has been nominated for a Nobel Peace Prize for his humanitarian work.

www.DrRademaker.com

WAKE UP YOUR COURAGEOUS SELF

Neecol Resnin

I s there anything or anyone that is intimidating you today or trying awfully hard to do so? Are there people, circumstances, or even the voices in your head that are making you timid or downright fearful, so much so that you desire to retreat, stay small, or give up?

Maybe you work or live with someone who intimidates you. Around them, you feel like you don't have a voice or that what you offer isn't valuable. Change the channel. Listen to a different message. Take a stand.

As a child, living in a tough neighborhood, I was often intimidated or scared. I rarely felt safe or protected, especially against the bullies in my neighborhood.

We had big trees in the neighborhood, and in the summer, caterpillars would fall from the trees or the boys would climb up to get them. With a fistful of these creepy crawlers, the boys would grab the girls and stick the furry insects down our shirts, shove them in our hair, and laugh as we hysterically screamed, "Stop! Stop!"

Each summer this would happen; there was no let up. To try to get them to stop, we would do anything. Using our fear, these boys would demand that we give up the little candy money we had, make us go to the store and buy them things, and have us sweep their backyards; we were treated like their slaves. And we did everything they asked—anything to avoid having caterpillars crawling down our backs. Eventually, just saying "caterpillars" would be enough to cause us to do whatever they wanted.

One day, I had had enough, and I made a decision. I don't know where this came from, but I decided I wasn't having this anymore. No matter how much I hated to have caterpillars put down my back, I was not going to run anymore. I was no longer going to give these boys the satisfaction of watching me squeal, run away, or do what they wanted. It was one of the first moments in my life that I realized I had power and I was done giving it to them.

That day I was shaking on the inside, like a 10.0 earthquake. Intention is one thing; action is another! I announced to the caterpillar bullies, "I am not running. I am not afraid of the caterpillars."

The lesson of my stand against the caterpillars is that I do not have to run from my fear. Over and over I would be reminded of the caterpillar wars, and I would delight at the memory of the confusion and shock in the eyes of those big, bad boys when I refused to play their game.

These bullies tried me a few more times, but I didn't back down. Those moments of courage, those moments of calling forth my own power, changed things for me and for them. It wasn't long before they no longer bothered me.

And it turns out, courage is contagious. The other girls now looked up to me, and some of them gained enough courage to challenge their bullies and meet their fears. When they did, they no longer had to go through this year after year either.

You too can acknowledge that "I am afraid of this thing" but then decide that you want to be on the other side of it all. You too can say, "I want to conquer this fear." Perhaps you are dealing with your own creepy caterpillars, and like me, you have no one to protect you or make them stop. Maybe the voices in your head are threatening you in some way, causing you to fear stepping out or taking a stand.

That's okay. I had allowed the caterpillars to be placed on my arm, back, or anywhere the boys wanted to throw them, and my first step to escape that was to take control of what I could—my reaction. I had no way of knowing what would happen, but I survived. I was willing to take the risk. My self-respect was worth it.

You too must confront your fears. Who criticizes you? Who is telling you, "You do not have what it takes to make it"? Don't give others power over you. Embodying someone else's thoughts or opinions of you can and will limit your vision of your life. It will keep the bullies laughing at you and make you run from a life of self-worth and self-acceptance. It can keep you from having a life of fulfillment.

Don't allow bullying thoughts (yours or others) or the fear of being judged or criticized by others to convince you that you do not have what it takes to succeed. It is never too late to take a stand, to be courageous in the midst of your fears. Don't give up. Don't give in. You will be stretched, but you will win.

How I chose to act at the time when the bullies grabbed me and put caterpillars down my shirt and in my hair was a moment of transformation for me. Just as a caterpillar transforms into a butterfly, I transformed from fear to freedom. No longer was the caterpillar a symbol of shame and intimidation but one of respect and power.

You have a courageous self within you too. Stand up and be accounted for.

Your choice can bring transformation to you—and to others watching you. Your life *does* matter. Your visions and dreams do matter.

I once read that the process going on within the cocoon that transforms a caterpillar into a butterfly is truly amazing. Once wrapped up tightly, the caterpillar literally melts down into a liquid, during which time they only retain the starting points for their most important features, including their eyes and wings.

There is a butterfly inside of you waiting to grow wings and fly. You may be encountering some challenges right now, and you may not see wings or the means to overcome. But be determined to not allow others to scare, stop, or crush your spirit. Stand your ground. By doing so, you are standing up for yourself. You can overcome your fears, develop your wings, meet the challenge, and became a hero to others who also have the same fears.

If you have to melt down to a liquid, retaining only the drive and vision inside your heart and soul, do so! Be your courageous self, and your wings will surely come.

Neecol Resnin, president and founder of Born for More, is a powerful motivator, woman of faith, author, teacher, and speaker. Neecol uses personal life stories to impart that no matter what one is facing or how outrageous one's dream, there is always a way to overcome any adversity. Neecol's will to survive and ever-consuming passion to help others find their path to recovery and beyond is unquenchable. Neecol believes that your past pain can propel you toward your purpose. Through coaching, speaking, and leading workshops, Neecol inspires and equips people to overcome anything, have faith in God, and develop an inspired action plan. She gives hope to the hopeless through her well-developed skills and strategies for success. Neecol holds two master degrees, one in business and one in clinical psychology.

www.BornForMore.com

TURNING A PENCHANT FOR SECRETS INTO A CAREER

Judy Schriener

Ever since I was a little kid, people have been telling me their secrets. I'm not sure how it started. The first time it made an impression on me that maybe I had a special gift for getting people to tell me their innermost thoughts and secrets was in high school. A neighbor girl in one of my high school classes invited me over to her house one day and told me about some of her adventures. I listened attentively, didn't interrupt her, asked her a few "how" and "why" questions, and I nodded a lot. Afterward, she looked at me with a puzzled expression and said, "You're not shocked, and you're not judging me." In the decades since, I've heard that over and over. That and, "I've never told anyone this before."

From early, early childhood, I've been a curious person. Yes, I want to know how things work. But mostly I want to know how people think and feel. I live to know how people think and feel. I live to learn who people are behind their public façade and why they do things.

After college, I went into advertising as a career. I worked for two ad agencies, I wrote ad copy for clients of a radio station, I sold radio time, I sold graphic arts services, I ran an in-house advertising agency for a large car dealer, I managed advertising for a large real estate company with seventeen offices, and I was the Director of Advertising for the Arizona Lottery, the first lottery west of the Mississippi, when it launched.

In each of those stints, I got close to the people I dealt with, whether they were colleagues, clients, or vendors. They told me amazing things about themselves, from the moment one knew his marriage was over, to how a woman pulled off cheating on her husband without his knowledge, and then one man showed me pictures of himself indulging his obsession with cross-dressing. (The secrets weren't all about sex but, after all, that's where a lot of secrets lie.)

Then a divorce—mine—nearly brought me down, both personally and career-wise. I needed a change.

I saw an ad for a writer/reporter for a small weekly business newspaper in Phoenix, Arizona, where I lived. I'd never written for a publication, but I knew I was a good writer, a fast learner, a thorough and detailed researcher, and I knew I could get people to talk to me. I got the gig.

The way I learned to write for publication was that I turned in my stories and when they ran, I went over them line by line to see what my editors had changed. Soon they weren't changing very much at all.

Best of all, I got people to talk to me. I was truly interested in them as people. I could easily read people when we were face to face, but I was scared to do interviews over the phone, which I had to start doing when I interviewed people outside Arizona. Amazingly, I could hear so many clues over the phone—how they breathed, when they hesitated, what they emphasized—that soon I could "read" them at least as well over the phone.

That little writing gig led to a thirty-year career in journalism, where I got paid—sometimes well paid!—to indulge my curiosity and get people to talk to me. I've lived and worked in New York City and Washington, D.C., I've written a professional book that McGraw-Hill published and sold for sixty dollars each, and I've traveled all over the world.

I chose business journalism because I wanted access to the best minds in business rather than "the public." Business people—executives and entrepreneurs—are among the smartest and most optimistic people in the world. And I've gotten to interview literally thousands of them over the years. Some were celebrities—they have ties to business, too—and nearly all were accomplished, successful people. Business people are generally very accessible to journalists. If they didn't want to talk, I would tell them, "We're going to do a story on you/your company either way, and we'd rather do it with your input." In some very unlikely cases, I got my interview by saying that, but mostly I got the interview by referring them to other people they respected who vouched for me.

Keeping people's secrets became a way of life. People told me things that could send them to prison if they got out. They ratted on each other and sneaked me confidential documents, and I had to keep to myself who they were. I told people, "I'll go to jail before I'll reveal that you're my source." I never had to go to jail, but I remember how excited I was when one company threatened to sue me if I used a document they didn't want to get out. "I'm doing something important, or they wouldn't want to sue me!" I thought. I used it. They didn't sue me.

Over the years, I've written countless stories and profiles of people who run companies. Mostly, people trusted me and told me the whole story. I urged them to tell me sensitive details "off the record" and then got many of them to permit me to use those same details "on the record." They trusted me to be fair.

I got awards and recognition. What was more important to me was getting access to the people I wanted to talk to and getting them to open up to me. I've gotten great info and insight from people I was told would never crack. And nearly all talked to me multiple times afterward.

I've never aspired to be on radio or television. "The delete key is my best friend," I'd tell people. But things change. I have hosted a radio show, *Off the Record with Judy*, for upward of four years. Every show is chock full of secrets, personal and professional, and I've interviewed many successful people and a handful of celebrities all around the world. Mostly, I just get interesting, successful people to open up and share their secrets. I live for that, and I've gotten paid to do just that for the last thirty years. How lucky am I?

Judy Schriener is an award-winning journalist, author, and radio show host who has interviewed thousands of executives and entrepreneurs in her thirty-year career. After writing a business book published by McGraw-Hill, *Building for Boomers: Guide to Design and Construction*, she is now focusing on writing books about relationships.

www.OffTheRecordWithJudy.com

HOW DESPAIR INSPIRED
MY LIFE'S WORK

Susan Sheppard

In 1983, I was lonely, sad, and confused. I had just turned forty, and it seemed like my life was in a shambles. We had lost our homes to foreclosure, both the investment property and our family home. The business partnership that I had considered to be solid was suddenly dramatically brought to an end, and we were about to be homeless, broke, and unemployed. What went wrong?

My despair was noticeable. We were both intelligent, educated, and capable, and yet we were staring into the face of marital, financial and emotional disaster. We loved each other, but that wasn't enough. We weren't getting what we wanted at all. We needed help.

I sought counseling for Viet Nam veterans' families. Bob, my husband of seventeen years, had been a Green Beret who served for two years in Viet Nam. I really didn't know about his tour, because the subject had been completely off limits.

During twenty-five PTSD (Post Traumatic Stress Disorder) screening questions, I agreed that he didn't beat me and he wasn't a drug abuser. The other questions about nightmares and sleeping with a gun under his pillow and inability to stay employed and contempt for authority struck me in the heart, and I realized we were living in a world outside the realm of normal. The nurse paused, then suggested that I must be a strong woman. I was crying. I had been doing crisis intervention as an RN in Emergency Services since age twenty, and I could not save us.

Our family went to the Viet Nam Vet Center a few times, but Bob was unwilling to talk about the war and refused to return. The girls, ages fifteen, twelve, and five, were rebelling against any kind of counseling. I was very frustrated, and I still didn't completely understand his issues. Finally, I gave him an ultimatum that he either use his three degrees to get a teaching job or get out.

Bob taught for three years, but when he ignored the district rules, the administration dismissed him. Then after a three-year construction project, both he and the Marine veteran who owned the construction company were waiting for work to appear.

I started to tell Bob I was leaving him, and he interrupted the conversation to make a phone call. I took that personally. I didn't realize it was his way of coping. My heart was broken, and I did what I usually did when things didn't work out, which was to take every course I could find to learn. This time it was about relationships. I wanted to know how to love, be classy, and still get what I wanted.

I loved Bob but I couldn't fix this situation. I just didn't know what to do. My two oldest daughters were living on their own. Bob and our youngest stayed in the house, and I went to live alone. The day I left I spent 24 hours vomiting and crying. I filed for divorce. Bob never acknowledged our divorce, and it finalized two years later without his signature.

So far this story sounds like failure, not success, but there is more to the story.

After the divorce, I met and was dating a charming man who was eighteen years younger, foreign born, and the eldest of seven children. To make matters worse, his mother and I were the same age. Our romantic relationship didn't survive, but we remained very close friends. He resumed dating his younger girlfriend. I was able to observe their very dramatic two-year courtship as his friend and her "enemy rival for his attention."

Toward the end of that two years, she asked to talk to me. I responded, "Why? You don't even like me." Admitting to that, she said, "I have decided that he is not what I want. I have been watching while I have been his girlfriend and you have been his friend, and he is different with you than he is with me. It is like I have had his body and you have had his soul, and I want to know how to do that with a man. Will you teach me?"

I was shocked and said no. She persisted for several months until I agreed to a short-term coaching trial. Ultimately, this young woman became my first relationship client. We spoke daily for the next two years. During that time, I shared my story and everything I had learned to help her get what she wanted. I realized it was more fun to talk about love and sex than crisis intervention.

I developed my Love with CLASS system, which is even more perfected today. In the past twenty-five years, I have successfully coached hundreds of singles to get what they want in the way of a relationship. The young woman, now a dear friend, is still successfully married to someone she had known, but couldn't "see," before we expanded her perception of men.

As for me, I learned to turn my personal disaster into my life's work. I learned that I am a healer and an influencer and that my experience and knowledge offers hope to people with broken or wounded hearts. I learned that I make a difference and that my clients "trust me more than they are afraid" to own their personal power, expand their comfort zone, and grow.

Although I didn't save my own marriage, Bob and I remained very close friends and parents to our three beautiful daughters until his sudden death in 1999. If I had known in that first seventeen years of marriage what I know now about relationships, things might have been different for us.

My company is called Getting What You Want. As a life coach specializing in relationships, I use my Love with CLASS system to heal wounded hearts, grow self-esteem, teach personal power and to ask for what you want in a way that you will be heard. I'm still saving lives, but now I save hearts as well.

Susan Sheppard is a professional speaker, author, coach, and creator of Getting What You Want, Inc. Susan speaks to singles who want a relationship about men–women differences, raising self-esteem, and getting what you want in life. Susan is healing one relationship at a time with her unique Love with CLASS system.

www.GettingWhatYouWant.com

BE CAREFUL WHAT YOU ASK FOR

Dr. Jay Shetlin

In 2002, I was driving home from the world's largest annual chiropractic seminar, held each year in Las Vegas. My world had just been rocked by successful doctors, philosophers, authors, and political leaders! I couldn't wait to outgrow my successful little chiropractic clinic and start making a global impact. I even envisioned speaking someday on the very stage I just left. Driving home I had a conversation with God and asked Him to help me positively impact the lives of more people in the world through chiropractic, nutrition, and positive thinking.

Be careful what you ask for—because the means to the end you seek are rarely predictable. At least that was the hard lesson I had to learn before I would truly have the tools necessary to help the masses.

In hindsight the lesson unfolded this way . . .

It was as if the Universe opened up *The Book of Life Challenges* and threw several chapters at me all at once. Over the course of the next two years, uninvited surprise after surprise hit me, my family, and my businesses.

The Loss

My family's world was turned upside down: We went from living in our dream home, living in a quaint town, having a growing practice and booming second business . . . to losing *everything*! Our fourth child was born and developed cerebral palsy, an employee embezzled over $30,000 from one of my businesses and stole my identity, ruining my credit. My software crashed at my chiropractic office, which lead to a slow death of the practice. Someone even bought our office building and kicked us out so they could take our office space for themselves. After a year and a half of extreme trials, I was pretty much a broken man.

Crushed . . . frustrated . . . broke . . . depressed. I could see the writing on the wall. Creditors were coming after me and my personal assets, and I was running out of options. My two businesses, business partners, employees from both companies, and even strangers like the new landlords had left me vulnerable, exposed, and accountable for more problems than I could handle. I became very bitter. I felt like I had failed as a husband, father, and businessman. I had foolishly trusted others, thinking we would all take care of each other. I was angry at the world and especially at those who I thought had a direct hand in putting me in this position. I was at a point where I would have to file bankruptcy.

In the interest of brevity, I will just say that we sold every worldly possession we owned at garage sale prices or lost it. I mean *everything*! If it didn't fit in two airplane-ready suitcases per family member, we no longer owned it. We left town, humbled and humiliated. The "big city" of Salt Lake was simply not far enough from the pain and frustration I was feeling. But a ray of sunshine emerged. An opportunity had fallen in my lap to take the family to Portugal to work with an amazing doctor in a place that offered a fresh start and new opportunities.

The Comeback
Portugal was a hospital for my soul. I spent the next two years serving the Portuguese people with chiropractic care, having adventures with my family, and healing from the stresses of the past two years. I woke up early every morning to exercise, study scriptures and self-help books, and I even began writing my first book.

The Wake
One morning, while running along the beach at 5:00 a.m. and listening to an audio book by Dr. Wayne Dyer, he said something pivotal that struck me to the core. To paraphrase, he mentioned that most people have some major event (an injury, divorce, loss of a family member, etc.) that negatively affects their lives. Then they "anchor" to that for the rest of their lives as "the excuse" not to succeed or to stay miserable. He went on to say: "That is like sitting on a moving boat looking back at the wake and saying, 'Look at that wake; my life sucks because of it.' But the wake has nothing to do with where the boat is going! Stop living in the past and live in the present. Looking ahead to your future with optimism. You are at the helm."

Bam! I literally stopped in my tracks to soak it in. I had been crippled by the past two years' experiences, but I couldn't let those trials continue to hurt my present and my future. These words flipped a switch in my head.

Forgiveness
I still had a paralyzing "hang up" from the past. I was carrying around some deep-rooted hatred for the people I thought had played a part in my loss. Like so many of us do, I was blaming others for my misfortune.

I had an epiphany that I could not move forward personally if I did not forgive those that had wronged me. I needed to give up my anger, hatred, and bitterness for true forgiveness. The negative feelings I had for others were clearly holding me back from freedom and success. The perpetrators probably had no idea how I felt, and if they did, it still had no impact on their lives. But it was having a major debilitating effect on my life.

So I gave up. I turned it over to God. I said, "Lord, I forgive them for what they did to me. Maybe they know how much their actions hurt me and my family, and maybe they don't! Regardless, I will no longer let this affect me and my family. I take responsibility for the part I played in getting to this point. I love and forgive them as fellow children of God. I understand that we all make mistakes. God, I will let you be the judge of their actions. You can provide justice in this life or the next. It is not my place to judge others. I can't fully understand their circumstances. So, I am forgiving and I am moving on."

In that moment, I felt an overpowering sense of relief. But let's face it, we are human, and we typically think many of the same thoughts today that we thought yesterday. I needed to change my thinking permanently. I had to do more than just mutter the words one time. I prayed often. I meditated and did affirmations. And I had a sincere desire to let it go. Slowly my thinking changed.

With time, I was made anew! Empowered with the right mind-set, I could take the fuel of adversity to begin the journey of leadership in my family, my practice, my community, and the world.

Twelve years after driving home, inspired to help more people find success and happiness through chiropractic, nutrition, and positive thinking, I spoke from that very stage in Las Vegas at the same seminar where my journey began. Be careful what you ask for—you might just get it. But the road can be more difficult than you expected. Mine was brutally painful . . . but I wouldn't change a thing.

Dr. R. Jay Shetlin is known as "Utah's Premier Auto Accident Injury Rehabilitation Specialist." Dr. Shetlin founded the South Jordan Chiropractic Center and is specially trained to diagnose and treat distress in the musculoskeletal and nervous system. He provides chiropractic treatments that allow the body to heal naturally.

Dr. Shetlin has been amazed with the human body and what it's capable of doing ever since he was a kid. In his youth, his mother was injured in a car accident and sought chiropractic treatment. The therapy restored her health and vitality, leaving a lifelong impression on him that drove him into the field of chiropractic care.

www.DrJayShetlin.com

bryo. And the one egg that was fertilized competed with 400 to 500 other eggs to become "the dominant one" that resulted in Positively Powerful You! You were literally conceived powerfully. We are born unique, and we spend most of the rest of our lives trying to be like everyone else. Break out of the mundane mold—believe and become the positively powerful you that was meant to be.

You may ask, "How can I feel and ultimately believe that I am positively powerful?" I'm glad you asked. Follow these simple steps based upon the words *positive* and *powerful*.

P – Pause for Perception and Different Personalities. Begin by asking yourself the powerful questions at the beginning of the chapter. And remember that people see the world differently due to their perceptions and their own reality. How do your perceptions agree and differ?

O – Objectivity and Ownership. View your situation, whatever it may be, from an objective viewpoint; look for the positives. Take ownership for what you are accountable and responsible for and objectively assess what others' perceptions may be based upon who they are.

S – Stakeholders and Success Strategies. What is the impact of the decision you will be making? Who are the stakeholders to be affected? Employ positivity in the strategies that you will use to achieve success—yours, your team's, your family's, whomever the stakeholders are.

I – Invite Intuition and Imagine Outcomes. There is evidence to prove that our intuition is a viable decision making tool once we learn to trust and use it effectively. "Your knower knows." Trust the still, small voice. Imagine: visualize, feel, experience a positively powerful outcome. Be in that moment of realization, and keep it in mind as you move toward your goal.

T – Talk and Transact. Faith without action is dead. You can complete all the previous steps, but if you don't talk to the person or people and transact whatever business is at hand, nothing will ever change. And the goal is to be positively powerful! Talk! Transact!

I – Implement with Integrity. You've made it through the most challenging part. Now, whatever it is that you or you and others have agreed to do, actively implement it with integrity. Commit and execute with the power of positive intentions.

V – Verify. Follow through and follow up on your commitments. If you've encountered resistance or have begun to fall back in old ways, adjust and re-implement with integrity.

E – Evolve. The more you commit to following the Positive Approach through educating yourself and others, checking your ego, and encouraging the positive, the more quickly you will evolve into Positively Powerful YOU!

Perception
Of
Worth   ⬅⬅⬅POSITIVELY POWERFUL YOU!
Effecting
Reality
Favoring
Unlimited
Life

When your perception of your self-worth becomes positively powerful, when you know that you are a unique human being with unique gifts, and when you become fearless in the pursuit of using those gifts to bring joy to yourself and others, the odds are favoring unlimited life—your positively powerful unlimited life. If you knew you couldn't fail, what would you attempt? What are you waiting for?

It doesn't have to be hard.

Every conflict or loss of power that any of us have experienced in our lives occurred because we allowed it. That premise, while difficult to read and possibly even more difficult to accept, is a truth. We always have a choice—are we to be positively powerful or are we to shirk from our authenticity and the freedom and joy that it brings? Even in the delivery of less than pleasant news or when making a tough decision, choose the positively powerful course of action. That means that you will have to be true to who you are, navigate the terrain with wisdom and humility, and still make the decision that will ultimately be of the greatest benefit.

One of my greatest life lessons that I like to share to empower others came on the evening of my mother's passing. As I went to sleep that evening, I asked God to let me see her one more time, to talk to her, to be with her. As I dreamt, I got my wish. She appeared to me, her golden tiger eyes shining brightly, and she smiled at me and said these positively powerful words: "Honey, it doesn't have to be hard." I asked her "what" didn't have to be hard; what was she talking about? She just looked at me and smiled, repeating the phrase as she faded away.

What I have come to learn, in those life-blessing seven words, is that "it" is whatever we are facing. We choose. Will it be easy or will it be hard? When you begin to think, *I can't do this; it's just too hard,* I'm going to invite you to substitute the thought, *This is challenging, but I am positively powerful, and I will try.*

What are you making hard in life? You always have a choice, so choose to be Positively Powerful You!

A LIFE RE-ENGINEERED

Alan Skidmore

What do you want to be when you grow up? This is a question asked of young folks throughout the generations. And me? Well, I had originally wanted to be a doctor. That was my plan until I entered college; however, after spending a year as a biology major, I realized that maybe I was on the wrong track.

It has been said that whatever you are interested in during your early teens is most likely your true calling. My interests had been music, electronics, and gadgets, so I decided that maybe I should become an electrical engineer. After a multitude of technical classes and a ridiculous amount of math, I earned my coveted EE degree.

For the next thirty years I had a successful career as an electrical engineer, working in the automotive manufacturing, chemical, natural gas, and cable TV industries.

Not long after graduation, I married Penny, and within a few years we had two sons, Justin and Jesse. While my mom and dad had instilled a good work ethic in me, I eventually discovered that work becomes less about passion and more about a need to provide for a growing family. That's not a bad thing, but no one ever tells us this early in our lives. I suppose if we were told the truth, most of us would stay home and live with our parents forever.

Around the time I was thirty, I began listening to a lot of personal development programs and started attending seminars to learn what is not taught in the normal school curriculum.

A major shift in my life came around the time I turned fifty. I wasn't afraid of turning fifty, nor was it all that big of a deal; yet, when I stopped to think about it, I would wonder, "Where did the years go, how did I get this old already, and what I have been doing?"

During my fiftieth birthday party, which included black balloons, a stuffed crow, and birthday cards jokingly telling me that I was "over the hill," I had an epiphany. I told everyone that I was not over the hill, but that my fiftieth birthday was "the first day of the second half of my life!"

I decided then and there that I was going to have more fun in my life, which started almost immediately, though my life up until that time had certainly not been dull!

During my forties, I had become involved with Toastmasters International to learn how to be a better public speaker. From this training and because I wanted to share my knowledge, I began to speak at different events. In 2010, I was asked to speak at a technology conference in Melbourne, Australia, and again in Las Vegas. During that summer, just for fun, my youngest son and I went to Ghana, Africa, with a group from our church to help improve an orphanage that we supported. That was a life-changing experience, and I learned that the whole world was not like the United States.

My son and I also learned that kids can be happy with just the basics, and that all we really need is a roof over our head, clothing, food, and to share our love with others. And one of the best ways to improve your life is to discover the gifts that you have been given and then use those gifts to make the world a better place.

Just a few months before my fiftieth birthday, I was laid off from work for the third time in less than ten years. At this point, I was fed up with the corporate world and decided to work for myself and opened shop as an IT consultant. Also around this time, I attended my first RockStar Marketing Bootcamp with Craig Duswalt, where I met Glenn Morshower (Aaron Pierce of *24*) and numerous other Hollywood movies and TV shows), who has become a dear, close friend and a "brother from another mother."

By joining a group of like-minded people who wanted to make the world a better place, I discovered some of my gifts.

For me, that happened by becoming involved in the RockStar MasterMind program and taking many of the ideas learned from some great minds and applying them to my own life and business. Since then, I have grown my IT consulting business where I have more work coming to me than I can handle. As a result of one of these IT projects, I was offered and accepted a position as the IT Director for West Virginia State University. I certainly didn't see that one coming!

Then, really stepping out of the "norm," in 2013, I launched an Internet radio show called *Prime Time Success Radio with Alan Skidmore*. This adventure allowed me to share wisdom with folks from all over the world and to interview some very well-known experts, including Bob Burg, Dan Miller, and "The Pitbull of Personal Development," Larry Winget.

Over the past five years, I have traveled nearly around the world, met numerous rock stars and celebrities, and made friends with some of the most amazing people on earth. How did I do this? I changed my attitude, I decided that I was going to have more fun, and I stepped up and said "yes!" to all those opportunities that have appeared right in front of me.

I am often asked, "How does a country boy from West Virginia get to meet all these wonderful folks and do such cool things?" I tell them to step out, get on a plane, or jump in the car . . . and go!

You can get to just about anywhere on earth within twenty-four hours. So do something out of the ordinary. Turn off the TV, get off your smartphone, and stop watching other folks live their dreams. Go live your own! Move out of your comfort zone, get uncomfortable, and take a chance. Decide that you are here for a reason, discover that reason, and then pursue that mission with great passion!

Alan Skidmore is an IT and business consultant who speaks around the country and internationally. He is the co-author of *Choices*, author of *Don't Take Your Gifts to Heaven*, and the host of *Prime Time Success Radio*. He lives in West Virginia with his wife and two sons.

www.AlanSkidmore.com

POSITIVELY POWERFUL YOU! IT DOESN'T HAVE TO BE HARD

Melinda Stallings

Who are you? Answer that question with what automatically comes to mind. Don't stop to filter the answer. Most people will give the most obvious of answers: mom, dad, sister, brother, a man, a woman, a child, a husband, a wife, an attorney, a caregiver, an executive. And while you may indeed be one or several of these things, this is not "who" you are. Those are merely the outward appearances of a much more powerful being.

Owning that you are positively powerful means that you must answer the initially posed question as well as subsequent questions. What drives you? What frustrates you? What angers you or makes you sad? Why? What makes you happy (this being one of the most challenging questions to answer because happiness is so fleeting). What brings you great joy? Do you continually do things that you dislike? If so, why? What are the characteristics that you like about yourself? What are your unique gifts that you bring to the world? Do you like/love yourself? Why?

Once you answer these questions, you will begin to discover your authentic self. And your authentic self is positively powerful. Why? Because with authenticity you honor those gifts that are uniquely yours. When you honor your gifts and use them for humanity, you will discover that it brings you extraordinary joy. And when you have extraordinary joy, it brings great freedom. Freedom from facades, freedom from the back and forth of who you are and who you think you need to be for others, freedom to choose as you please because you are in every sense "honoring" your God-given unique gifts. Uniquely yours, like your thumbprint or the retina in your eye or the amazing fact that there will never be another person exactly like you—in all the billions of people on this planet, you are positively powerful in your uniqueness. Authenticity = Joy = Freedom.

Consider this: You are a miracle. Between 200 to 600 million sperm competed for the opportunity to fertilize the egg that resulted in your em-

and accountable for more problems than I could handle. I became very bitter. I felt like I had failed as a husband, father, and businessman. I had foolishly trusted others, thinking we would all take care of each other. I was angry at the world and especially at those who I thought had a direct hand in putting me in this position. I was at a point where I would have to file bankruptcy.

In the interest of brevity, I will just say that we sold every worldly possession we owned at garage sale prices or lost it. I mean *everything*! If it didn't fit in two airplane-ready suitcases per family member, we no longer owned it. We left town, humbled and humiliated. The "big city" of Salt Lake was simply not far enough from the pain and frustration I was feeling. But a ray of sunshine emerged. An opportunity had fallen in my lap to take the family to Portugal to work with an amazing doctor in a place that offered a fresh start and new opportunities.

The Comeback

Portugal was a hospital for my soul. I spent the next two years serving the Portuguese people with chiropractic care, having adventures with my family, and healing from the stresses of the past two years. I woke up early every morning to exercise, study scriptures and self-help books, and I even began writing my first book.

The Wake

One morning, while running along the beach at 5:00 a.m. and listening to an audio book by Dr. Wayne Dyer, he said something pivotal that struck me to the core. To paraphrase, he mentioned that most people have some major event (an injury, divorce, loss of a family member, etc.) that negatively affects their lives. Then they "anchor" to that for the rest of their lives as "the excuse" not to succeed or to stay miserable. He went on to say: "That is like sitting on a moving boat looking back at the wake and saying, 'Look at that wake; my life sucks because of it.' But the wake has nothing to do with where the boat is going! Stop living in the past and live in the present. Looking ahead to your future with optimism. You are at the helm."

Bam! I literally stopped in my tracks to soak it in. I had been crippled by the past two years' experiences, but I couldn't let those trials continue to hurt my present and my future. These words flipped a switch in my head.

Forgiveness

I still had a paralyzing "hang up" from the past. I was carrying around some deep-rooted hatred for the people I thought had played a part in my loss. Like so many of us do, I was blaming others for my misfortune.

I had an epiphany that I could not move forward personally if I did not forgive those that had wronged me. I needed to give up my anger, hatred, and bitterness for true forgiveness. The negative feelings I had for others were clearly holding me back from freedom and success. The perpetrators probably had no idea how I felt, and if they did, it still had no impact on their lives. But it was having a major debilitating effect on my life.

So I gave up. I turned it over to God. I said, "Lord, I forgive them for what they did to me. Maybe they know how much their actions hurt me and my family, and maybe they don't! Regardless, I will no longer let this affect me and my family. I take responsibility for the part I played in getting to this point. I love and forgive them as fellow children of God. I understand that we all make mistakes. God, I will let you be the judge of their actions. You can provide justice in this life or the next. It is not my place to judge others. I can't fully understand their circumstances. So, I am forgiving and I am moving on."

In that moment, I felt an overpowering sense of relief. But let's face it, we are human, and we typically think many of the same thoughts today that we thought yesterday. I needed to change my thinking permanently. I had to do more than just mutter the words one time. I prayed often. I meditated and did affirmations. And I had a sincere desire to let it go. Slowly my thinking changed.

With time, I was made anew! Empowered with the right mind-set, I could take the fuel of adversity to begin the journey of leadership in my family, my practice, my community, and the world.

Twelve years after driving home, inspired to help more people find success and happiness through chiropractic, nutrition, and positive thinking, I spoke from that very stage in Las Vegas at the same seminar where my journey began. Be careful what you ask for—you might just get it. But the road can be more difficult than you expected. Mine was brutally painful . . . but I wouldn't change a thing.

Dr. R. Jay Shetlin is known as "Utah's Premier Auto Accident Injury Rehabilitation Specialist." Dr. Shetlin founded the South Jordan Chiropractic Center and is specially trained to diagnose and treat distress in the musculoskeletal and nervous system. He provides chiropractic treatments that allow the body to heal naturally.

Dr. Shetlin has been amazed with the human body and what it's capable of doing ever since he was a kid. In his youth, his mother was injured in a car accident and sought chiropractic treatment. The therapy restored her health and vitality, leaving a lifelong impression on him that drove him into the field of chiropractic care.

www.DrJayShetlin.com

bryo. And the one egg that was fertilized competed with 400 to 500 other eggs to become "the dominant one" that resulted in Positively Powerful You! You were literally conceived powerfully. We are born unique, and we spend most of the rest of our lives trying to be like everyone else. Break out of the mundane mold—believe and become the positively powerful you that was meant to be.

You may ask, "How can I feel and ultimately believe that I am positively powerful?" I'm glad you asked. Follow these simple steps based upon the words *positive* and *powerful*.

P – Pause for Perception and Different Personalities. Begin by asking yourself the powerful questions at the beginning of the chapter. And remember that people see the world differently due to their perceptions and their own reality. How do your perceptions agree and differ?

O – Objectivity and Ownership. View your situation, whatever it may be, from an objective viewpoint; look for the positives. Take ownership for what you are accountable and responsible for and objectively assess what others' perceptions may be based upon who they are.

S – Stakeholders and Success Strategies. What is the impact of the decision you will be making? Who are the stakeholders to be affected? Employ positivity in the strategies that you will use to achieve success—yours, your team's, your family's, whomever the stakeholders are.

I – Invite Intuition and Imagine Outcomes. There is evidence to prove that our intuition is a viable decision making tool once we learn to trust and use it effectively. "Your knower knows." Trust the still, small voice. Imagine: visualize, feel, experience a positively powerful outcome. Be in that moment of realization, and keep it in mind as you move toward your goal.

T – Talk and Transact. Faith without action is dead. You can complete all the previous steps, but if you don't talk to the person or people and transact whatever business is at hand, nothing will ever change. And the goal is to be positively powerful! Talk! Transact!

I – Implement with Integrity. You've made it through the most challenging part. Now, whatever it is that you or you and others have agreed to do, actively implement it with integrity. Commit and execute with the power of positive intentions.

V – Verify. Follow through and follow up on your commitments. If you've encountered resistance or have begun to fall back in old ways, adjust and re-implement with integrity.

E – Evolve. The more you commit to following the Positive Approach through educating yourself and others, checking your ego, and encouraging the positive, the more quickly you will evolve into Positively Powerful YOU!

Perception
Of
Worth   ←←←POSITIVELY POWERFUL YOU!
Effecting
Reality
Favoring
Unlimited
Life

When your perception of your self-worth becomes positively powerful, when you know that you are a unique human being with unique gifts, and when you become fearless in the pursuit of using those gifts to bring joy to yourself and others, the odds are favoring unlimited life—your positively powerful unlimited life. If you knew you couldn't fail, what would you attempt? What are you waiting for?

It doesn't have to be hard.

Every conflict or loss of power that any of us have experienced in our lives occurred because we allowed it. That premise, while difficult to read and possibly even more difficult to accept, is a truth. We always have a choice—are we to be positively powerful or are we to shirk from our authenticity and the freedom and joy that it brings? Even in the delivery of less than pleasant news or when making a tough decision, choose the positively powerful course of action. That means that you will have to be true to who you are, navigate the terrain with wisdom and humility, and still make the decision that will ultimately be of the greatest benefit.

One of my greatest life lessons that I like to share to empower others came on the evening of my mother's passing. As I went to sleep that evening, I asked God to let me see her one more time, to talk to her, to be with her. As I dreamt, I got my wish. She appeared to me, her golden tiger eyes shining brightly, and she smiled at me and said these positively powerful words: "Honey, it doesn't have to be hard." I asked her "what" didn't have to be hard; what was she talking about? She just looked at me and smiled, repeating the phrase as she faded away.

What I have come to learn, in those life-blessing seven words, is that "it" is whatever we are facing. We choose. Will it be easy or will it be hard? When you begin to think, *I can't do this; it's just too hard,* I'm going to invite you to substitute the thought, *This is challenging, but I am positively powerful, and I will try.*

What are you making hard in life? You always have a choice, so choose to be Positively Powerful You!

Hailed as a visionary and thought leader in positive influence, Ms. Stallings masterfully created "The POSITIVE Approach" a principled approach born professionally of reducing conflict in organizations yet it positively applies in personal interactions as well.

She is an energizing conference keynote and breakout session speaker, organizational improvement consultant and professional executive coach. She travels internationally spreading the core message of positivity whether discussing self-discovery, leadership, change, communication, strategic planning, conflict resolution or a variety of relationship building topics.

www.MelindaStallings.com
www.ThePositiveCoach.com

CONSTRUCTING A SUCCESSFUL BUSINESS

Barbara Starley

I love entrepreneurs and small business owners. I love their passion, their drive, and their tenacity. They've put it all on the line—their time, their energy, and often their life savings . . . literally their blood, sweat, and tears—to start their business. They move into the entrepreneurial space excited, inspired, and motivated to go out on their own.

At the beginning things look pretty rosy. They are doing what they love. They are their own boss. Nobody is telling them what to do or controlling their schedule. They may not be making a ton of money, but it's okay . . . for a time.

It usually doesn't take long for them to realize that there is a lot to know about running a business. Their excitement turns to confusion, their inspiration turns to lack of direction, and their motivation turns to overwhelm as they try to figure it out on their own and keep up with the many functions of running a successful business.

According to Bloomberg, eight out of ten entrepreneurs who start a business fail within the first eighteen months. Not for lack of trying—but often for lack of good, solid information.

In many cases, small business owners have no one to come alongside them and point out the pitfalls that await them or caution them about the authorities that will pursue them—relentlessly—if they mess up.

The real problem is that most entrepreneurs and small business owners simply don't know what they don't know.

They don't understand cash flow.

They don't understand profitability.

They are lying to themselves (and possibly to the people they love the most) about how well they are doing.

They are afraid that one day they will receive a big, thick envelope from the IRS demanding either an audit or money—or both.

They've heard that they shouldn't be paying their employees like indepen-

194

dent contractors, but everyone in their industry seems to be doing it, so they assume it must be OK.

They buy the QuickBooks® program, but there it sits—untouched. Or worse, they attempt the setup on their own and then throw their hands up in frustration. Not because they aren't capable—but because they have no guidance.

Many business owners will go (or send their employees) to a one- or two-day QuickBooks® training, but that can be time-consuming, overwhelming, and too generic for their particular business.

More than twenty years ago, my heartstrings pulled me into the small business community where I met incredible entrepreneurs and small business owners who were completely underserved in accounting and finance. They were confused and needed help, but they had few people to turn to. These small business owners generally had little money to spend on high-priced consultants and even less time to try to figure it out on their own.

I believe small business owners are the backbone to our economy, and their success will ultimately benefit generations to come.

I've had the honor to serve more than a thousand small business owners and entrepreneurs, assisting them to lay a firm foundation by getting things right from the get-go . . . or clean up the mess they've gotten themselves into.

Recently I had the pleasure of chatting with Patty Aubery, president of The Canfield Training Group, who spoke to my heart when she said, "Look at how many clients you have helped beat the odds of failure. You are like the Suze Orman of small business." Wow!

My mission is simple: I empower entrepreneurs.

I do a lot of the "dirty work" that other consultants won't do, and at times I've had some tough conversations with my clients.

I've cleaned up messy books so that my clients' tax preparers could not only prepare accurate tax returns but, more importantly, give my clients good tax advice as well.

With my proven system, I've trained bookkeepers who failed every accounting class they ever took, hate math, or were thrown into the bookkeeping position unprepared and against their will.

I want my clients to succeed, and I want their in-house staff to not only know what they are supposed to do, but understand why their job is so important. Whether that bookkeeper stays with that company for years (as many of them do) or eventually moves to a new position, that person is more equipped and more valuable in the marketplace.

Because I believe that integrity honors God, I've challenged my clients to build a business of integrity. Integrity starts with being informed. In accounting, integrity includes reporting all earned income as well as paying employees, vendors, and taxes on time. It includes being realistic about time commitments and available resources. Integrity is also about using each person's God-given talents to construct a business that gives the world the best of who they are.

Over the years, it has been gratifying to watch my clients create amazing businesses that support their families, strengthen their communities, fulfill their dreams, and contribute to their favorite charities.

Much like the clients that she serves, Barbara Starley constructed her own successful business from the ground up and in such a way that allowed her the freedom to control her schedule and to be at home to raise her son.

Barbara is a Christian, Certified Public Accountant (CPA), Certified QuickBooks® Pro Advisor, Certified LivePlan® Expert Advisor, Member of the Intuit® Teacher/Writer Network, speaker, author, wife, and mom.

Barbara does QuickBooks® setup, training, and troubleshooting for entrepreneurs and small business owners (on-site and virtually) and serves as their On-Call Controller™ on an as-needed basis.

www.BarbaraStarley.com

My Journey as a New Hybrid Publisher

Karen Strauss

Twenty-five years in business . . . publishing pro—I have worked at major houses such as Random House, Macmillan, Crown, and Avon. I started Strauss Consultants to work with traditional publishers to give them an equal level playing field to get them into large chain stores: Barnes & Noble, Borders, Books A Million, Walmart, etc.

I started Strauss Consultants in 1991, and I had a blast doing this new thing on my own and helping smaller independent publishers sell more books and really play with the big boys. Interestingly enough, my primary clients turned out to be Christian publishers who really needed this nice Jewish Girl from New York's help. It was awesome being part of a revolution in bringing Christian books into the mainstream.

I got to sell fiction, nonfiction, and children's books and work with authors, publishers, and marketing people. As an entrepreneur I learned about all facets of publishing and helped my clients sell more books into a marketplace that had previously shunned them.

I was blessed—I had a really good run selling books and consulting with publishers to grow their revenue

Many years later in 2009, Borders goes out of business, independent brick and mortar stores start to close and Amazon starts to take over the world! What's a girl to do? I could see the handwriting on the wall. The publishing landscape was changing . . . and changing fast.

I knew I needed to figure out a transition for Strauss Consultants because selling books to brick and mortar stores was at some point not going to be viable.

In 2010 I had a major setback. I was diagnosed with breast cancer—which really crashed my world! That year was a whirlwind of doctor's appointments, tests, tests, and more tests, surgeries, more surgeries, repeat surgeries, chemo, radiation, hair loss—and finally a new breast implant, which tragically fails.

Were it not for the amazing support of friends, family, and a little dog named Izzy and a irritable but loving cat named Allie, I don't know how I would have survived. But that's a story for another day.

In 2011, finally recovering, I was getting back out there. But I was still faced with this nagging issue of flailing book sales, Borders being closed, and Barnes & Noble struggling. It wasn't a crisis yet, but I knew it would be sooner or later.

And then the idea came to me! I should start a publishing company! *Really? Am I possessed? How can I be different from everyone else out there? I know so much about publishing, but how can I leverage what I know? Can I really do this?*

Despite my fears, reservations, and doubts, Hybrid Global Publishing was born in 2012. It's for authors who want to expand their brand, increase their business, and get speaking engagements and publicity.

To be perfectly honest, after after years in publishing, this was the steepest learning curve I have ever had. It's been like trying to put together a very complicated seven-course dinner and make it all come out perfectly cooked—at the correct temperature and ready to be served at the exact time it needs to be on the plate.

Figuring out how to produce an author's book with editing, cover design, interior design, ebook, and distribution just like a traditional publisher would do is a massive undertaking. I've made a lot of mistakes! It was like a game of dominoes—I lined up the pieces and then, if one fell apart, the whole production fell apart. I went through vendor after vendor trying to put together just the right team who understood how hybrid publishing worked. I know hybrid publishing is the pioneer zone of publishing, so not many people were familiar with this model. People know self-publishing, such as Create Space, and they understand traditional publishing . . . but hybrid publishing is a new breed.

I am proud of the fact that I am one of the first people in this space and am making it a respectable publishing option for serious authors.

If you are thinking about writing a book, I seriously encourage you to write one. Here are ten reasons why.

1. Demonstrate your expertise.
2. Increase your credibility and status.
3. Solidify and articulate your knowledge.
4. Expand opportunities for media and speaking.
5. Create multiple streams of income.
6. Grow your business.
7. Differentiate yourself.

8. Launch a business (an online webinar series or a course).
9. Gain more customers.
10. Change your life.

I am honored to have worked with over 300 independent authors, many of whom have gone on to be extremely successful in bringing their business up to the next level.

Karen Strauss has worked in publishing for over thirty years at Random House, Macmillan, Crown, and Avon. She is publisher of Hybrid Global Publishing and enjoys working with independent authors. Karen is the author of *Book Publishing for Entrepreneurs: Top Secrets from a New York Publisher.*

www.hybridglobalpublishing.com

FROM CODEPENDENCY
TO "INDEPENDENCY"

Scott Transue

Growing up in a highly dysfunctional, addicted household can be brutal. You learn the three rules for survival very quickly: Don't talk, don't trust, and don't feel. Those rules work well while you're a child and not yet responsible for your own life. They are outright dangerous rules to live by as an adult.

I kept living those rules into early adulthood, and paid the price. One abusive relationship after another, getting stuck in "dead-end" jobs, and not getting promoted into higher-skilled positions. It all culminated when a total nervous breakdown struck, the result of stress from the unrealistic demands of a dysfunctional workplace. I wound up in the hospital for a week. Quite frankly, I had lost the will to live. I did not care anymore.

I was released from the hospital and started on a path of intense therapy. Deep inside, I knew I was on earth to do something special. After all, there must have been a reason for all the pain I had experienced. As destiny would have it (I no longer believe in "luck"), I located a company on the Internet that advocated for adults dealing with trauma. I inquired, and spent three years with them as a work-from-home advocate.

With a newly-found sense of self-esteem, I was browsing LinkedIn once day and noticed a profile for a recruiter for a national seminar company. Mind you, I had been speaking for free with Toastmasters for years. The recruiter and I connected, and I asked whether they were looking for speakers. It was a question I would not have asked years before, thinking I was not good enough.

The recruiter said "Absolutely. Put together a video of you speaking to a group, and I will run it past our screening committee." I was simultaneously thrilled and scared to death. I had my Toastmasters club create the video for me and sent it in. About four days later, an email from the recruiter appeared. It read "Scott, call me. I need to discuss your video." I knew it . . . not good enough.

I called the recruiter and was asked when I might be available for an orientation call. "Orientation?" I asked. She said, "Well, yes. I thought you were interested in a speaking contract. Your video was one of the best we have seen this year." I almost dropped my cell phone. We scheduled a ninety-minute orientation call and finalized plans for me to fly to Kansas for meetings with key staff.

Fast-forward one year. I have now given seminars in over twenty-five states and have gotten contracts with three separate webinar companies. I have co-authored one book and have been a contributing author to another. Simply put, I feel like a RockStar, and it will only get better from here. I also now own two companies, a public speaking firm and a tax consulting firm.

I remember back to those extremely lonely days as a child and to that hospital stay that would change my life. I realize that God sometimes puts us into very negative circumstances so that we'll have something to share with the world as a result. After all, diamonds are created out of intense pressure.

So, if you need a speaker who can talk all about "making lemonade from lemons," I can help. If you need a very skilled tax professional, I can help. If you need someone to represent you or a loved one during the Social Security Disability process, I can help. If you know anyone who needs help in any of the above areas, contact me.

Even if you don't, however, remember the following. You're already great just as you are. No matter where you have come from, or what you have been through, you have something valuable to share with the world. Something no one else can share quite like you can. I found out what my message is. The only question is, what is yours? Once you figure that out, you will open up a world that, right now, may not even be conceivable for you. And maybe, just maybe, we can both share a stage and impact people around the world. So, when can we schedule your orientation call?

Scott Transue is a professional speaker, author, and tax professional. He presents seminars across the country on tax planning for small businesses and owns Freedom Day Tax and Accounting LLC.

www.ScottTransue.com

Minding the Gaps: Part Two

Jeffrey Wolfe

Lay down on your back. Look up. See that long wrench?"

"Yes."

"Grab it with your right hand. Use it to turn that bolt above you to the right."

A bright flashing light illuminated the part fastened by that bolt.

"That flashing light shows where there is interference."

"Have you built it yet?"

"No. Fortunately. In the real world, the service technician would not be able to access that bolt to remove it. That's a multimillion-dollar problem."

Standing up, I removed the "Virtual Reality" visor that enabled me to see and interact with a product and field service tools that were still only "engineering drawings" in a 3-D computer program.

"Without this Virtual Reality system, we couldn't find that until we wasted millions of dollars designing and building real products."

That was 1995.

In 2016 I thought about that experience while watching a TV commercial for a "Virtual Reality" visor for smartphones. Twenty-one years later, the technology we worked with had made it to consumer applications.

Today's state-of-the-art, already-in-the-field technology will be twenty years beyond the hottest "gee-whiz" technology available to consumers.

Stop. Read that again: Today's state-of-the-art, already-in-the-field technology will be twenty years beyond the hottest "gee-whiz" technology available to consumers.

Let that sink in.

A key insight gained from working with advanced technologies is this: *Today's "gee-whiz" state-of-the-art technology is twenty years behind what's already in the field somewhere in the world.*

How much has changed over the past twenty years?

Are you prepared for the next twenty?

What does that mean for you, your career, or your business? Apply this "thought exercise" to that question: You're currently twenty years behind your most technologically advanced competitor—how do you not only survive but thrive? AND— what "crazy-talk," currently unthinkable technology could revolutionize what you do?

That leads to another key insight: *Technology is not an end unto itself.* Technology enables, enhances, and accelerates.

Virtual reality helped change how products were developed because it allowed people to work together in ways that were considered impossible. Imagine being able to test drive a new car three years before it was built—*and* tell the car designers what to change if they expect you to buy one. How would that change your thoughts about what car to buy next? If the buttons on the radio were hard to see or reach, it would be possible to make changes before ordering the parts to assemble it. Anything you would like changed could be explained to the manufacturer before they built the car.

Technology, virtual reality in this example, interacts with our perception of what is possible. We were already thinking differently—way "out-of-the-box"—before applying the "tech." Once we applied the "tech," we were able to see new possibilities, literally getting out of the box. That led to even more radical changes in how we developed products.

Which leads to another key insight: *It's still all about relationships!*

Technology enables changing how those people interact and how the relationships work. In the mid-nineties I was involved with changing how we create new products, specifically aircraft and launch systems. Not just making better planes and rockets, but improving how they are being created.

We needed the right people in the right roles with strong working relationships because that allowed debating—sometimes loudly—about what would, could, or could not be done and then taking massive action together. Technology does not eliminate the need for strong relationships based on common vision, trust, and respect.

When disrupting how several thousand people work to earn a living for their families, emotions run high at times. At the extreme, I received death threats—delivered face-to-face—while working with a Fortune 500 company to implement disruptive changes affecting over 10,000 people. (Spoiler alert! No action was taken on that threat.) Having strong relationships with our team allowed for working through such emotional resistance rather than being derailed because we trusted each other as well as the team's mission.

Here's our final key insight for this discussion: *Change is like bungee-jumping off a bridge!*

Imagine climbing over the railing of a bridge, looking at the rocks 150 feet below you, and hearing your friends shout "Five, four, three, two . . ."

Just being on the "wrong" side of the bridge's guardrail makes every cell in your body scream "Nooooo!"

When influencing someone to change their work habits, perceptions, or thought processes, you invoke the same physical and psychological responses as they would experience climbing over that bridge railing. The intensity may not be as mind-numbing, but they experience it at some level.

This is true whether the change involves taking a different route home from work, using a different work process, or embracing a new faith. Only the intensity proves different.

"Change" may be the only true "given" in the Universe, yet most people do not experience it gracefully (myself included—but that's a whole book!). As we implemented changes, and applied the technologies that facilitated those changes, a lot people's roles were affected.

Allow time and emotional "space" for that effect when influencing people to make changes to their routines or perspectives.

These key insights will help you navigate "The Gap" discussed earlier. Surrounding yourself with people willing to discuss "what if" or "if the impossible were possible" creates a framework for that. The objective in doing so is *not* accurately predicting "The Gap." Here's a big secret: It's about finding ways to do today what's commonly considered "impossible."

Jeffrey Wolfe, CEO of AdventureCEO, creates transformational Adventure Summits for CEOs. He also speaks, writes, and trains on leading change, operational excellence, and strategy. Mr. Wolfe has worked with organizations such as the National Institute of Standards & Technology, Hughes Aircraft, Kodak, Gould Electronics, McDonnell-Douglas Corp., and the California Manufacturing & Technology Center. To discuss "The Gap," "what if," or other questions contact him at Info@AdventureCEO.com.

www.AdventureCEO.com

HAVE A NICE DAY, UNLESS YOU'VE MADE OTHER PLANS

Lori Zapata

Respecting and honoring my feelings has always been a challenge. It stems from spending so many years believing my feelings were secondary, or more accurately, last and unimportant. Even with simple decisions like what movie to see, I'd worry, "What if no one likes my suggestion?" How sad is that, to believe you are not worthy enough to pick a movie?

Feelings are never right or wrong. They are simply yours and need to be respected and valued. Now, while that is true, what you do with your feelings can end up being right or very, very wrong. Learning that lesson can be tricky. I had to learn to recognize my feelings and convince myself that mine were important. No longer could I put myself last. As I learned to identify what I was feeling, I became empowered to take action, even if that action was to sit still and just breathe. It required breathing deeply, through anger, as I became aware of the resistance you face when you try to stop being the doormat. Many people do not like change, even if that change is a positive one. Some will try to hold you back. Don't let them. Push forward.

It has been said that feelings follow thoughts. If you find that you always put others before yourself, you need to feed yourself with positive thoughts until you believe them, because . . . *you are worthy. Your thoughts matter. Your feelings matter. YOU MATTER!*

Motivational quotes can help snap you back when life pushes you off track. I find they give me strength. One of my favorite quotes is "If you believe you can, or if you believe you can't, you're right!" You must get rid of negative thinking and believe in yourself, or no one else will.

Be brave, and don't be afraid to fail. "Every failure is a lesson. If you are not willing to fail, you are not ready to succeed!" With hard times come opportunities to grow and lessons to learn. We all have our own journey. There will be tough times along the way and storms we must get through. Remember this: "Serenity is not freedom from the storm, but peace amid the storm." The secret is to love and value yourself, face your storms head on, look for the lessons, and learn to dance in the rain.

Over the years, I had quite a few life lessons to learn. As a child, I was a victim of sexual abuse. Much of what happened did not surface until I was an adult. All I knew was that I always felt less than everyone and everything. I tended to like people who were not nice to me. How bad was it? Well, I didn't realize that there was something wrong with my marriage when I drove myself to the hospital to deliver my first son. Nor did I see a problem with being told, "Call your sister," when I managed to crawl to a phone after collapsing in pain while six months pregnant with my second son. What? I even told my husband that our one-year-old son was running around the house and I couldn't get to him. He did finally come get me, but quickly left me along in the emergency room and went back to work. What's worse is, he was self-employed. I couldn't even pin this on his boss. After three days in the hospital with kidney stones, I returned home, happy that all was okay with my baby. The marriage . . . well, that was not okay. I did leave, but not for another two years. How low does your self-worth have to be to accept being treated like that?

"If you don't learn from history, you are destined to repeat it," so of course, after finally getting out of an abusive marriage, I dated another abuser. Again I stayed through many incidents. The craziest followed an evening out with friends. I came home to a ransacked apartment and a note that said I stayed out too late and that he would kill me. One might think that would be the breaking point, especially since he carried a gun. It wasn't. When I finally did leave, it wasn't over an incident. Through therapy, journaling, and positive thinking, I finally found enough self-love to walk away. Sexual abuse had stolen my self-worth, but I was finally learning how to take it back.

Today, I am happy. I'm the proud mom of two amazing young men. I have made mistakes raising my boys; I was always trying to shield them from all pain and disappointment, forgetting how important and necessary those life lessons are. As a mom, how do you let your children fall? However, we all have to fall, or how can we learn to get back up? It's still hard for me, and we are all still learning life lessons. Being a mom is my proudest accomplishment, and I hope my boys know how much they are truly loved.

My wish for you is that you take care of yourself and truly value your feelings. Put the best *you* forward, and it will improve every relationship in your life. It all starts with believing you are worthy and honoring the truth that your feelings matter. This is something you'll need to continually work on, or life will sneak up and put you through some lessons again. I've learned that the hard way.

I no longer accept unacceptable behavior. I truly believe that I matter and can do anything I set my mind to. I'm rebuilding my life and making my dreams come true. So can you! "Your mind is a powerful thing. Fill it with positive thoughts and watch your life start to change." A happy life is within your reach. Choose happiness, and choose to love yourself. Only *you* can "rock your life," so . . .

"Have a nice day, unless YOU'VE made other plans!"

Lori Zapata is a motivational speaker and #1 best-selling author featured in the book *Women Who Rock: Inspirational Stories of Success by Extraordinary Women*. As a Nikon professional photographer, moment chaser and memory keeper, Lori's photography has been seen in the *Chicago Tribune, New York Hockey Journal*, Broadway singer-songwriter Linda Eder's CD, *Linda Live*, as well as many other publications. Lori enjoys shooting everything from weddings to hockey and rock stars. She also enjoys teaching photography and sharing her passion while helping others follow theirs.

www.LoriZapata.com

CRAIG DUSWALT'S RESOURCES

Main Website
www.CraigDuswalt.com

Craig Duswalt's Rock Your Life Nights
2017 World Tour—coming to a city near you!
www.RockYourLifeNight.com

Craig Duswalt's RockStar Marketing BootCamp
Every March and September in Los Angeles
www.RockStarMarketingBootCamp.com

Craig Duswalt's RockStar BOOK Camp
How to Write a Book in 30 Days to Promote Your Business and Get it Published
Every May
www.RockStarBookCamp.com

Book Craig Duswalt as a Keynote Speaker
www.CraigDuswalt.com

Speaker Bureau
RockStar Keynote Speakers
www.RockStarKeynoteSpeakers.com

Shopping Cart
www.RockStarCart.com

Click Funnels
www.RockStarClickFunnels.com

Craig Duswalt's RockStar MasterMind
Elite community where "RockStars" exchange ideas to grow their Business and succeed in Life!
Come to any of Craig Duswalt's events to find out more about this exclusive membership.

Craig Duswalt's Speaking Topics

Corporate:
How to Achieve *RockStar Status* in Your Industry
RockStar Motivation & Inspiration
RockStar Marketing
RockStar Leadership

Entrepreneurs:
How to Achieve *RockStar Status* as an Entrepreneur
How to Write a Book to Promote Your Business and Self-Publish It in 30 Days

Colleges:
How to Achieve *RockStar Status* in College *Without* Doing Drugs

To book Craig Duswalt as a speaker at your next event, please call 805-241-8170.